Stop the World, We Want To Get On

By Ann Reed and Marilyn Pfaltz

Stop the World, We Want To Get On

Ladies Who Lunch

Your Secret Servant:
Fix and Freeze Hors D'Oeuvres
for Easy Entertaining

Stop the World, We Want To Get On

Ann Reed

and

Marilyn Pfaltz

Charles Scribner's Sons   New York

Library of Congress Cataloging in Publication Data
Reed, Ann.
  Stop the world, We want to get on.
  1. Women in the United States.   2. Women—History
and condition of women.   3. Vocational guidance for
women—United States.   I. Pfaltz, Marilyn, joint author.
II. Title.
HQ1426.R42   301.41′2   74-11047
ISBN 0-684-13980-4

1 3 5 7 9 11 13 15 17 19 V/C 20 18 16 14 12 10 8 6 4 2

Stop the World, We Want To Get On is dedicated to today's women. It is a call to confidence for the women who recognize the options and opportunities of the present, who are eager to face the challenges of the future, and who are committed to expanding the dimensions of their lives.

Contents

Stop the World, We Want To Get On

Chapter *I*

One Rainy February...

Marilyn's Story

*M*y first recollection of wanting to be someone or do something was in sixth grade. Our class was assigned the task of writing "My Autobiography." I recall that my two ambitions were to be a harpist and a writer. Several years of piano lessons and the accompanying struggle of daily practicing discouraged any dreams of playing the harp. However, thoughts of writing for publication were never far away throughout the intervening years.

As an English major in a liberal arts women's college, I was ill-prepared to enter the job market after my graduation in 1954. I did not want to teach, and the only other job opportunities available were as secretary or girl Friday in the publishing world or in an associated field. The myth propounded by personnel departments in those years was that there were lots of future career possibilities, but they all entailed a secretarial apprenticeship. Four college years of stimulating research and study were now put to use in a crash course of typing and shorthand. As a result I secured a job with a major advertising agency in New York City.

Since many classmates became engaged during my senior year, and even more married in the first year after college, I think I was secretly relieved to meet and marry my husband within two years of graduation. I was offered a challenging new position in the agency about the same time as our engagement. In turning down the offer, I had two distinct feelings. First I felt a sense of excitement and anticipation in embarking into marriage. There was no doubt in the minds of my friends, my family, or myself that "occupation: wife" was the ultimate in careers for women. My second feeling was a momentary sense of loss for the job that might have been. However, such thoughts were quickly overshadowed by the thrill of wedding plans.

My early married years were mobile and interesting. The first six months were spent as a Navy wife stationed at a large air base. Then my husband entered law school, and we spent three relatively carefree years enjoying the company of other student couples. The routine of being a housewife did not begin until we were settled in a community where my husband entered private law practice. Our family meanwhile had increased by the addition of three children. Young children are physically time consuming, and there were very few hours then when I was free to wonder what else I might be doing.

Probably the only moment such a thought crossed my mind was when I received my college "Bulletin" and read about my fellow alumnae who all seemed to be writing books and holding important jobs. A small owl symbol appeared in the "Bulletin" pages next to the announcement of someone's significant achievement. I privately vowed that someday this owl would herald my book's publication. At that time, however, my inclination was not strong enough and my involvements with house, children, and community seemed all-consuming. Occasionally I bought a copy of the "Writer Magazine," but I never put pen to paper and followed through on any of the ideas which swirled in my head.

I held many volunteer jobs through these years and received a sense of accomplishment by working on a variety of projects. I gained self-confidence in recognizing my own abilities and limitations. My husband meanwhile was successfully pursuing his chosen profession, and he encouraged me to expand my interests and horizons. For more than ten years home, husband, and community activities absorbed most of my life. Thoughts of "what to do next" seldom filled my mind. "Next" seemed forever in the future.

Soon my youngest child entered first grade, and I discovered what seemed like hours for myself. "Next" suddenly became "today" as school years began to fly by. Every year there seemed to be more free hours in each day. Tennis games, bridge, committee meetings, and trips to the supermarket, not to mention cleaning and recleaning my house, were not a full-time occupation. I frequently entertained vague thoughts of someday finding something to do. The confinement of a full-time job was not too appealing after years of doing things on my own schedule. I really didn't envision myself away from home all day. However, I began to buy the "Writer Magazine" regularly and daydream more often about short-story ideas.

One rainy February . . .

Ann's Story

I think I always wanted to be a doctor, at least from elementary school onward. I had a favorite sixth-grade teacher who introduced me to the world of biological sciences. I was fascinated with all things medical, and my first dreams were of becoming a veterinarian. By the time I was eleven I was continually finding stray birds, cats, dogs, and other animals to bring home for nursing.

High school considerably broadened my scientific horizons. I developed a special interest in chemistry and biology, and medical school beckoned. After school and during the summers I spent many volunteer hours at a nearby hospital pushing carts and working at the snack bar. As I roamed the hospital corridors, my fantasies exchanged my candy-striped uniform for a doctor's white jacket.

I attended a liberal arts women's college and majored in

zoology. During these four years my goal gradually shifted from an M.D. to a Ph.D. in medical research. I had become increasingly interested in scientific investigation and enjoyed the challenge of exploration. Probably a truer reason for modifying my ambitions was the appearance of a special young man in my life. I realized that medical school and the time commitment it necessarily demanded was considered to be incompatible with marriage, or so it seemed in 1957. When I became engaged during my senior year in college and married six months later, I abandoned thoughts of a professional career with no regret and barely a backward glance. After all, marriage was the fulfillment of every woman's destiny, according to family, friends, and all current magazines and movies.

My first half year of married life was spent as a service wife living alone while my husband completed his tour of duty. Fortunately my four years of liberal arts had given me a marketable skill, and I went to work in a nearby laboratory. For three years I worked as a research assistant. Nonetheless, I was pleased to retire at the birth of our first child. The possibility of a Ph.D. became more and more remote as I ran after first one and then two small children.

In 1964, a year after its publication, I read *The Feminine Mystique* as an assignment for a neighborhood book club. As I recall, an afternoon's discussion of the book did not trigger any response in me. I don't remember sensing any identification whatsoever with Betty Friedan's "mystique" or for that matter feeling one bit guilty that I was only a housewife. However, it must have left a latent spark, because during those early married years whenever I filled out a form requesting my occupation, I hesitated writing in the word "housewife." I usually wrote "housemanager."

I was happy with my roles of wife, mother, and volunteer. As my babies grew into toddlers, I became more involved in volunteer activities. I was exposed to interesting community services and enjoyed the opportunity to direct and administrate. As the years passed, thoughts of someday going back to college reappeared in my consciousness, although I reasonably decided the elusive Ph.D. was just not in the cards. However, with my background and interests, medical library work occurred as an interesting possibility. I went so far as to make a phone call to a nearby hospital inquiring about its library and what qualifications were necessary for its personnel. A library science degree was indeed a prerequisite. The problems of fulfilling graduate school requirements seemed too complicated at the moment.

One rainy February . . .

*O*ne rainy February, over a cup of coffee, we were both discussing our over-involvements in organizations and committees. We agreed that we were happily pursuing our activities but that demands on our time always seemed to pull us in a million directions at once. We idly speculated about "doing something." The idea of gathering our energies together and finding a challenge away from our world of bake sales and car pools was appealing.

Amidst much laughter we spent the morning inventorying our marketable skills and talents. It wasn't a very long list. However, we had a delightful time fantasizing what we might do with a few extra hours from our week. By our own immodest admissions one thing we did do rather well was cook. We both enjoyed entertaining large and small groups and preparing gourmet specialties for appreciative guests. The small members of our families still preferred their hamburgers straight. We were eager to find any excuse to serve more exotic fare. Why not write a cookbook?

Just articulating the thought gave a sense of possibility to the idea. Several days passed, and our idea seemed more and more attractive as we discussed it. We approached our husbands for their reactions, and they surprised us with their immediate and wholehearted endorsements. They each had heroically suffered through all our kitchen experiments of early married life. As our cooking improved with practice, they had become more discerning about food preparation, and they enjoyed tasting and testing recipes. They appreciated eating good food and were prepared to sample every experimental meal.

Our off-the-top-of-the-head remark, "Why not write a cookbook," became a reality. We had spent a few hours debating whether we should and scarcely a few minutes discussing whether we could. It was an exciting challenge to tackle something new, and we were off and running with the purchase of two notebooks and some paper. We swore our families to silence. For fear of being teased by our gourmet class–attending friends, we began our book in secret. It did seem presumptuous for two housewives without authors' credentials to announce to friends that they were writing a cookbook.

Our first problem was to decide on the type of cookbook. We did not want to compete in a subject already covered by a well-known author, or to write the fourth fondue cookbook currently on sale in every bookstore. After pouring over the subject index of all cookbooks in print, we discovered that there were no recent books on hors d'oeuvres. It was a perfect subject for us. Hors d'oeuvres are creative cookery, which we enjoyed. It did not demand fancy French cooking skills, which we did not possess. Furthermore we both thought feasting on hors d'oeuvres for the next months would be more interesting than our usual family menus.

Where did we find the recipes? We first sorted through our own collections, which seemed to shrink on close inspection. Next we went to the library and spent hours looking for ideas and suggestions with which to experiment. Up to this point in our cooking careers we both had naively assumed that a recipe disaster was obviously the fault of the cook. But from disastrous experience, we found that the written word could be incorrect. Misprints are understandable, but clearly impossible directions are shattering to the cook. Once we spent three hours trying to fill a tiny pastry tube made around a pencil mold. On paper, cheese cigarettes sounded like a great idea. However, nothing short of magic was going to put a thick filling inside a cigarette without having it crumble into pieces. Since there were two of us trying to follow the instructions, we were sure by the end of this session that the recipe was unworkable as written.

As we continually discovered inaccuracies in many cookbooks, we gained confidence in our own judgment to select and write recipes. Our secret bookwriting was exposed one afternoon when a friend stopped by at our kitchen. Cookbooks, papers, pots, and pans were piled high on the counter. She jokingly asked, "What are you two doing, writing a cookbook?"

"Yes," we answered somewhat tentatively. For the first time we were forced to commit ourselves publicly. Her enthusiasm was immediate, and surprisingly it never seemed to occur to her to doubt our abilities. From that moment we had to take ourselves more seriously, because now our friends expected a cookbook from us. It was a little like being pregnant, only it took more than nine months to produce a manuscript. Those months were filled with solicitous friends irritatingly asking when they could buy the book. If nothing else their continued questions prodded us into coming to grips with the essence of the book we were writing.

Most significantly, we evolved a theme around which to develop a book out of our collection of recipes. We became convinced that hors d'oeuvres preparation was often neglected by a harassed hostess while she frantically cleaned her house and planned a dinner menu. Hors d'oeuvres establish an initial impression, because they are the first food guests will sample. Since first impressions are lasting, great care should be taken to impress. We adopted the idea of fixing and freezing everything in advance in order to give the hostess time for fussing over garnishes and serving pieces as well as allowing her a relaxed time during which to prepare the meal. As we began to write we were forced to define and refine our style. We decided that all recipes must be easy to fix and elegant to serve. Their written directions must be simple to follow and very short.

We decided that in order to test our recipes and theories we would give an enormous party for two hundred of our nearest and dearest friends. For days beforehand we fixed and froze fifty varieties of hors d'oeuvres at our "leisure" between meetings, drivings, dinners, and dishes. Our guests were given a tally on which to record their likes, dislikes, and general comments. The party was a smashing social success, but all we learned was that people's tastes vary. For every guest who loved the ginger cheese ball, there was another who suggested politely (or not so politely) that we leave it out. However, the general idea of a frozen hors d'oeuvres cookbook was well received, and our food offerings were consumed with enthusiasm.

From the beginning of our cookbook idea, we, as a team, were always confident of our eventual success in producing a published book. Whatever momentary doubts either of us may have had privately, by unspoken agreement, we never communicated them to each other. Our party supplied a final boost of confidence, and shortly thereafter we finished the manuscript.

The moment of truth had arrived. Up to this time we were merely two housewives who said they were writing a cookbook. Just as a writer of plays is not a playwright until a play is produced, an author becomes an author only upon publication. To become an author we were going to have to submit our ideas to professional scrutiny. We took our initial step into the business world the day we mailed our manuscript to our first would-be publisher. Our agonies of decision, hours of reading, cooking, typing, and eight months of more or less managing to maintain an unruffled household while writing a book all boiled down into a package that could be mailed for twenty-four cents.

In retrospect mailing our manuscript was a gigantic step. We were finally putting ourselves on the line, risking either failure or success both in our own eyes and those of our families and friends. One might have thought that such an important step would have caused some second thoughts, perhaps even hesitation or reluctance to step out into a competitive marketplace away from the security of husbands, children, and loyal supporters. Quite the contrary, our only serious concern at the time was the type of folder which would be suitable for our opus. We didn't even know what a manuscript binder should look like. We spent at least an hour in a large stationery store trying various binders on our precious papers much to the amusement of the salesmen. The fact that we were about to place our self-image blithely in the hands of the publishing world somehow escaped us.

Our search for a publisher was a real ego test. Fortunately there were two of us, and we never faltered in our belief that our book was marketable. Our attempts to communicate with any New York City publishing office became our biggest frustration. When we placed a call to someone of "importance" in one of these firms, the first person (and we may add usually the only person) we spoke with was that "someone's" secretary. It quickly became apparent that suburban housewives were a category of third-class citizens to most secretaries. Everyone in the office was either "not in yet," "at a meeting," "out to lunch" (which lasted two hours), or had "just left for the day." Getting through this forward line of defense was the first of our many obstacles.

We had always agreed that the demands of our families would come first, but at this time by some sleight of hand we were determined to convince both potential publishers and our families that they were uppermost in our thoughts. This juggling wasn't easy.

A perfect example of our recurring dilemma was an experience with a prominent woman editor who had very kindly consented to see us at ten o'clock one Wednesday morning. Late Tuesday afternoon the editor's secretary called us, "I am sorry to have to change tomorrow's appointment to three o'clock. Is that convenient?" Honestly, our answer should have been, "It is absolutely impossible, because of children coming home from school, no babysitter, and miserable city commuting traffic which probably will make us late for dinner." However, without a moment's hesitation, we indicated three o'clock was just fine, so that our potential editor would never doubt our business-like attitude. Dozens of telephone calls later we managed to arrange our lives at home so we would make our appointment. We arrived breathless but prompt and were shown immediately into the editor's office. Our editor was standing with her coat over one arm, an overnight case in the other. She greeted us apologetically, "Hello, so nice to meet you. I do apologize for having to rush off, but I have a plane to catch. I will take your manuscript with me and will be in touch when I return." We were back down on the street and into a restaurant sipping a cup of tea within ten minutes of our arrival. It was a letdown, to say the least, after building high hopes for such a meeting. Together we could laugh at our machinations to keep our three-minute appointment. However, we had avoided the evening commuter traffic, and we were home in time to prepare dinner and meet our husbands. Everything happened for the best, we supposed.

It was unsettling to receive rejection slips. Again, thank goodness there were two of us. We had absolutely convinced ourselves that our book was good, that there was no comparable book available, and that it would be a valuable addition to any cookbook shelf. Letters from publishers accompanying the return of our manuscript never indicated that our manuscript was unpublishable, only that they couldn't use such a book right now. We believed every word.

About this time even our most interested friends pointedly no longer asked, "How is the book coming?" Our receipt of several rejection slips dimmed their picture of us as real authors, and they were kind enough not to want to bring up an embarrassing subject. Little did they know what we in fact were doing. We had learned that it was difficult to describe the intricacies of finding a publisher to those who were not involved. It was a completely new experience for us, and it was impossible to translate to others.

Mostly out of curiosity and just a bit seriously, we investigated a publisher who advertised that it was reading original ideas which it would publish in "financial cooperation" with aspiring authors. When we arrived at this particular office, we were slightly taken aback to find the firm located three elevator stops over a taxidermist's shop in a part of New York City generously described as "deteriorating." Certainly the company was not wasting its profits on appearances. We were eagerly welcomed by the receptionist and shown into a semi-elegant conference room which had wall to wall bookshelves presumably filled with the firm's successful publications. Moments later a charming vice president joined us to discuss our book. He enthusiastically took our manuscript and assured us that we would hear his decision within ten days. Merely as a footnote, he produced a typical contract which he gave to us to read. "Financial cooperation" apparently meant that authors paid for three-fourths of a book's printing and distribution costs while the publisher paid for one-fourth. The contract's royalty clause assured a profit to the publisher of the book. If the book did well or if it did poorly no one would be much out-of-pocket except the author. Needless to say we received a letter of acceptance in less than ten days. We really were not as innocent in the ways of contracts and finances as might have appeared, and we did not seriously consider this choice. Self-published authors are not acknowledged as legitimate in the eyes of booksellers. However, it didn't hurt to have an ego boost along the way, wherever the source. Our warm reception and serious author-publisher discussion remain a fond memory.

During one of our encounters with another editor, it was suggested that if we found a "premium sale" for our book, any publisher would be glad to print it. She explained that book premiums were popular with many companies for advertising purposes. All those coupons which people clip and never mail for dishes, appliances, and books are premium offers. Although not completely discouraged by the publishing business' apparent failure to recognize the merits of our book, we decided to try a new direction. We took up the pursuit of a premium sale.

We first searched through several supermarkets, looking for likely companies whose products were used in hors d'oeuvres. We made a long list of cheeses, instant drink-mixes, paper products, specialty gourmet foods, and other related items. Our next step was to contact manufacturing firms to sell them on the idea of using our book as a promotional piece. The secretaries who defend the entrances to these businesses were even more formidable than those who protected the publishing industry.

One morning we arrived bright and anxious in a premium office. We approached the secretary guarding the entrance and gave our names. She looked at us absolutely blankly and asked, "Where are you from?" "Summit, New Jersey," we chorused. "What does that company make?" she asked. It was obvious we had problems of communication.

Dozens of trips, phone calls, and letters later, we found a company which was interested in using our book as a premium. As it happened we were simultaneously offered a contract by a well-established publisher which we refused. This refusal needs some explanation to those wondering if we finally had cracked under the strain of trying to get beyond the front desk secretary. The contract which we received seemed to require us to be responsible for more than the publisher. It proposed a very small royalty payment and suggested that the publisher's staff was going to take over the final moments of creation for our book. We quickly discovered that unpublished authors are not considered experienced enough to give many opinions. After all our months of work we had a great many opinions to give. Since we already had a guaranteed premium sale, we decided to publish the book ourselves.

In retrospect, innocence and ignorance were our two greatest assets which allowed us to believe that we could succeed in any undertaking. Our volunteer experiences had fortunately given us a conviction that a task tackled was a task accomplished. Having spent four years at college learning to organize our minds and define objectives, we were mentally prepared to embark on a challenge, at least theoretically.

It was now about a year from that original rainy February morning. Our families were eating regularly, still wearing ironed clothes, and talking about "when that book would be ready." (Note the use of the word "when" rather than "if.") Both husbands gave us their wholehearted support and urged us to go into the publishing business. Although we did sit down and discuss the pros and cons of such a venture, these discussions always revolved around the central question "why not?" Probably if we had made a list of all the steps required and all the decisions yet to be made, we would not have dared to proceed on our own. Instead, our lawyer husband incorporated us and our banker husband set up the books. We were a business. Until this moment we had not allowed much of our "work" to spill over into our families' routines. However, going about the business of publishing a book involved more than just a few appointments and sending off a manuscript to await its return. Our "work" became more a part of our day, and our families became increasingly more involved. At our public library we found a volume entitled "How to Publish a Book." This book soon became our trusted friend and advisor.

We hired a freelance editor, located a manuscript typist, found an artist and layout expert, and selected a printer. We were constantly forced to make dozens of decisions as to print size, type-face, paper stock, page size, and cover material. Making decisions was something we always had done unhesitatingly. Housework was finished earlier in the morning to free the day for the business at hand. All our friends were puzzled by our apparent preoccupation, and, since there was no way to explain details, we became even more vague on the subject of "that book."

Almost another year flew by as we guided our book to publication. As the date approached when bound books would be coming off the press, we had to face one final obstacle. The premium books were sold but our problem was how to store and distribute five thousand extras which would soon be delivered to our houses.

We never doubted that there was a public anxiously ready
to buy our books. Our children helpfully suggested that they
would fill their red wagons and peddle them from door to
door. This did not fit our image of respectable authorship.
Our husbands did not look kindly on storing five thousand
volumes in our garages or basements. Obviously we had to
sell our finished product to some publishing firm. We were
completely unaware of how truly unlikely was such a sale.
Once again we recontacted publishing firms with a very positive approach. The closing sentence from our letter to them
read:

> We sincerely believe this book conforms to . . . high-
> quality standards and we could offer it to you for dis-
> tribution on a no-risk basis. This would give us the
> advantage of . . . distributional facilities and you would
> gain an addition to your list at no financial risk and every
> expectation of substantial profit.

We were obviously not troubled by lack of confidence in our
product!

To make several long months' story short, Charles Scribner's
Sons accepted the book, and we were asked to come in and
discuss arrangements. Our arrival was enthusiastically greeted
by receptionist and secretary alike. As we sat in a vice-presi-
dent's office exchanging pleasantries, he picked up the phone,
"We are ready for the conference now. The authors are in
my office."

Imagine how we felt. It made up for all those secretaries.
Two years of work was finally finished or so we thought.

That day in February when we started collecting recipes for
our "cookbook," we set a course of events in motion. Because
we had publicly proclaimed what we were doing, pride as
well as self-determination spurred us on when we suffered

disappointments or confronted apparent impasses. Our self-confidence never wavered, and we refused to doubt that we would accomplish what we had set out to do. Single-minded purpose of this sort probably is best described by the maxim, "Fools rush in where angels fear to tread." (We certainly were a pair of fools who rushed constantly into situations where knowledgeable angels would have advised us not to venture.)

"The more public appearances made, and the more publicity received, the more books would be sold." We took this promotional axiom to heart and organized our lives around it for the next year. We had stayed with the book thus far, and we realized no one would promote it with as much enthusiasm and interest as ourselves. A first book from brand-new authors launched into the highly competitive cookbook field needs a selling send-off. Our new challenge was to sell out the first printing of five thousand by Christmas.

A whole new world opened to us as we took to the lecture circuit. Up to this point we had operated out of our kitchens, writing and telephoning, with occasional half-day trips into the city. We still managed most of our volunteer activities and could be counted on for car pools as well as long chatty phone calls from friends. We were housewives busily engaged in writing and publishing a cookbook. Our first lecture while we sat nervously awaiting the program chairman's cue, "It gives me great pleasure," caught us in a state of shock. We had suddenly become "the guest speakers." All these people had come to hear us! In the eyes of our audience we were professional cookbook personalities. This was a new self-image, and it took awhile for us to get used to it.

We had most amusing adventures while the weeks flew by. We spoke to morning clubs, women's clubs, newcomers' clubs, luncheon clubs, book clubs, gourmet groups, library friends, and even appeared as a live "show and tell" for first graders.

We quickly learned that flexibility is the key to success when
you are demonstrating food. No matter how many phone calls
or letters were exchanged discussing the details of our appearance, when the appointed day arrived, it was inevitable that
some unexpected surprise awaited us. Microphones that "never
did that before" suddenly went dead. Platforms and tables
requested for the program vanished into air. A specific, carefully described request for an electric hotplate for cooking
food produced an electric tray for warming food. It is very
difficult to demonstrate how to cook crêpes on a warming tray.

We spoke before hundreds of people assembled in large
public meeting rooms as well as a dozen club women gathered
in a member's home. We spoke through thick and thin. At one
meeting in a large department store, we spoke in competition
with the gushing waters of a magnificent rococco fountain
located squarely in the middle of the room. This fountain not
only obscured our voices but the audience's view as well.
There was only one standing microphone for two of us, and
just to complete the acoustical debacle, the storewide muzak
could be heard playing softly in the background. How much
could be heard of what we were saying was questionable. No
matter, at the end everyone clapped like mad and bought a
lot of books. That, after all, was why we were there.

Even though club groups had often gone to great lengths to
secure us as guest speakers, there always seemed to be a problem of how to fit us in between the old and new business of a
membership meeting. Once we sat through an entire hour's
discussion to build or not to build a new clubhouse. The arguments raged furiously between opposing views, as the program
chairman ineffectually tried to interrupt. The president was
carried away by the stimulating discussion and eagerly kept
calling on each hand as it was raised. Finally she gaveled
everyone to order and prepared to dismiss the meeting. The
program chairman leapt to her feet with a wild determined

gleam in her eye, "Madame President, I want to remind you, we have speakers . . ."

The president, blushing crimson at her oversight, sat down mumbling apologies. The program chairman continued, "By way of introducing the authors to you, let me read from the introduction to the first chapter."

We sat spellbound by our own prose being read with such eloquence and watched with fascination as the audience of young mothers began to evaporate through the door, hurrying off to be home for school-aged children. When we did get the floor, we tried our best to be light, humorous, and informative in ten minutes for the handful of members left.

We found that we were most amusing when a group to whom we were speaking had indulged in cocktails before our program. These preconditioned audiences have been among our best. As a matter of fact one such luncheon at a restaurant unexpectedly served wine with the meal as well as cocktails before. Understandably the business of socializing and eating took longer than usual. We sat cooling our heels in the vestibule, receiving periodic bulletins as to what course was being served. When at last dessert appeared, we were brought in and introduced. When our first lighthearted story brought forth inordinate gales of laughter, we realized our audience was pleasantly, happily, but completely swizzled.

Our successes on the lecture circuit gave us confidence to take on the media.

Our radio experiences spanned three-minute spots, open-wire questions and answers, and hour-long interviews. We have appeared on our metropolitan area's largest station with an audience of thousands as well as on a small neighborhood station whose listening audience is probably a few hundred. On television we have been everything from center stage cookbook authors demonstrating recipes to extra guests invited along with a gag writer and a poet. Our friends may have glamorous images of us hobnobbing with famous personalities and being ushered in and out of studios as celebrities. Nothing could be further from the truth. One time we turned out to be a three-minute filler on a thirty-minute show after we had traveled an hour to get to the station and prepared elaborate food demonstrations as requested by the program's producer.

One of our more unforgettable experiences began when our publisher booked us on a full-hour interview show. We were given the interviewer's office address and told to report there one half hour before air time. The address was unnerving, since it was located in the middle of a city block surrounded by penny arcades, XX rated movie houses, and dance halls featuring all kinds of topless happenings. We seemed slightly over-dressed for the locale in our stockings, high heels, and white gloves. Ignoring curious stares, we found our building and took what appeared to be a shaky freight elevator to the correct floor. We stepped out into a long deserted corridor. Fortunately it had been raining outside, and we both carried sharply pointed umbrellas which we were prepared to wield. Without them we would have fled.

Around the corner we came upon a poorly lit room which was crammed with books and papers. A half dozen unshaven old men in floor-length tweed overcoats stood clustered in the doorway. With hearts pounding we went up and announced ourselves as the two cookbook authors. Nothing could have been more incongruous. A voice from within summoned us, and the men parted as we picked our way through the books to meet the "star." He was talking into his phone, barely nodding in our direction. The minutes ticked by, and for the life of us we couldn't figure out where the studio was hidden. Just like an old grade-B movie—we worried that maybe there really were white slave rings still operating in the Big City.

With a bang of the receiver our "star" whirled around to us and said, "Hi, girls. We go on the air in fifteen minutes. I didn't have time to look at your book, but the cover looks great. Write down six provocative questions and hand them to me at the studio. I'll meet you there. One of these men will walk you over." Before we could gather our wits we were back on the street headed toward the studio (we hoped), silently escorted by a sweet toothless old man.

The studio was a cavernous hall cluttered with cameras, lights, cables, and other electronic trappings. We were shown to a couple of empty card chairs, handed two cups of cool coffee, and told to be ready "to go on" in five minutes. There wasn't another female in sight, which did little to dispel our grade B movie impressions. A tall, esthetic-looking man with full flowing beard wandered in and eventually joined us. It turned out he was another guest. No one had even spoken to him, and he didn't know whether our interviewer had ever seen a copy of his book of poems.

By this time all pre-performance jitters had been banished by the insanity of the proceedings. With much humor we and the poet tried to imagine what could be "provocative" about hors d'oeuvres. We needn't have worried. The featured guest on the show now arrived. He was an old friend of the star, and they settled down on the set and chatted cozily of past antics for fifty minutes, give or take a few commercials. At last the authors and poet were brought on for the remainder of the hour-long show. It was now pouring rain, and inadvertently the terrible storm was mentioned. Since no one had read each others' books, the weather seemed the best topic to discuss for ten minutes. This kind of experience is hard to describe to friends whose mental picture of our celebrity status is so out of focus with reality.

Our book added a whole new dimension to our lives. Every family dinnertime was enlivened with Mother's adventures of the day. We had achieved a new status in the children's eyes, ever since one of them unexpectedly came upon our book on a shelf in the public library. Mother was an author! Both husbands were as proud of our success as we were and delighted in hearing about our daily happenings. Their continued pride was due in no small measure to our special efforts not to rock the boat. When we began accepting speaking engagements and autographing appearances, we tried not to disrupt our families' daily household routines. It was no small task to fit our public appearances into the private schedules of two husbands and five children. The gods have been good to us, and we have never had to make a choice between book and family. There have been several close calls, such as the day one of us was due at a business picnic and the two of us were scheduled for a booksigning. We prayed for rain, and it poured. "Everything works out for the best" is the maxim by which we lived.

Without realizing it we had slipped into a double life. First and foremost we managed to keep things at home running if not smoothly at least with as few bumps as possible. Once our husbands and children had left for work and school, we were ready to pursue our author-lecturer life.

It is a curious sensation to be lecturing before four hundred women who are hanging on your every word at 9:30 in the morning and at 2:30 in the afternoon to be gathering laundry from the hampers. There was no decompression chamber to help us in and out of our two lives. On one occasion a phone call served as well.

In this particular instance we had traveled several hours by car to speak to a club's annual luncheon. We had made caretaking arrangements at home, because we anticipated returning after dinner. Our appearance was a huge success and we sold lots of books. We were thrilled with everyone's pleasure in our book and feeling very much like successful authors.

Before leaving, we placed a call home to check on things. The phone was answered by the oldest of the five children. She assured us they were all together and everything was fine.

"What are you all doing?" we asked.

"We are all downstairs in the laundry room. The washing machine overflowed and there is water everywhere. We are mopping the floor."

What could we say? "Just keep mopping. We'll be home as quickly as possible."

As we raced homeward all too sure of the mess awaiting us, our speaking triumph at lunch had already become a memory. There was nothing like a cellar full of water to bring us back to earth!

On our promotional circuit, we were constantly asked if we were writing another book. People honestly liked the recipes and our point of view. We certainly didn't want to discourage a receptive public. We became accustomed to answering such questions with knowing glances and vague noncommittal answers, which gave the definite impression our next book was well underway. It wasn't.

However, about eight months after the publication of that first cookbook, we received a luncheon invitation from our publisher. We decided we had better come up with something to discuss. During the five-day lapse between his secretary's phone call and the appointment, we conducted a crash research program looking for a new idea.

It was an entirely new and pleasant sensation to be invited to lunch with our publisher. For us it was a far cry from being on telephone hold, long distance, while some secretary unsuccessfully tried to locate somebody who would talk to us. We were indeed asked for our suggestions for another cookbook. As if from off the top of our heads we casually mentioned luncheon menus as one possibility. On the spot it seemed to be well received, and we went home to await its final approval.

Even from the suggestion stage, writing a second book was a completely different experience from producing our first. There were no agonizing weeks of submitting a manuscript to a host of publishers and waiting months for their replies. Instead, a few days after our lunch, we were given the okay to proceed. Signing the contract for this book was no less exciting than for our first. Even so being handed a signed contract and a large advance check somehow is anti-climatic to the anticipation of the scene. Also we were well aware of the work ahead.

A deadline was agreed upon, and an editor was assigned to us. Back to the kitchen we went to taste and test for six months more. We had developed style and point of view the first time around which we continued. Our cookbooks were for a hostess who easily and elegantly prepared her food in advance so that she might calmly and graciously welcome her guests. As a footnote to our activities, since we began writing books, we have become frantic hostesses who seldom if ever entertain.

Because we had published *Your Secret Servant* ourselves, we had a great many notions about layout, design, and everything else. Our editor's infinite patience and wisdom was a large factor in the publication of our book as scheduled on time for the Christmas gift season. This last sentence conceals eight months of phone calls, visits, corrections, changes, suggestions, rewriting, and re-typing.

In the eyes of booksellers and public alike, authors of second books finally have a stamp of legitimacy. We were more business-like in our dealings and more professional in our appearances. We extended our travel area to several surrounding states. We limited ourselves to places which we could come and go from in a day's trip. Even though we might leave long before breakfast, we were usually home in time to cook and serve "easy and elegant" dinners. Husbands and children responded to our expanded careers and became very adept at getting each other off for work and school.

We were not only on the club lecture circuit but were initiated into the world of houseware demonstrators in department stores. These last engagements were always enjoyable, because it gave us a chance to shop. One typical morning we had arrived early as requested and set up a cooking table. We put two small saucepans of chocolate and butter on the waiting hotplate to melt. We had a good half hour to kill so we wandered off browsing through the store. It grew closer to lecture time and streams of women began filing by headed toward the demonstration area. As we stood near a cash register waiting to make a purchase, we were amused at the scraps of conversation we overhead about ourselves and our new book.

"That's funny, I think I smell something burning, don't you?" said one woman hurrying by.

Her companion agreed, "I sure do, and I think it smells like chocolate."

Good Lord. We had completely forgotten our pots on the hotplate! We left the poor salesgirl in mid sale and raced back toward the burning odor. We were mortified, much to the hilarious amusement of the gathering crowd. It was a great opening number for our cooking act.

We had many adventures, and our partnership bank account had begun to show a perceptible bulge. We vowed to stop our touring at the first sign of weariness with our own voices. Almost everywhere we spoke, women would come up to us after the program and inquire, "How did you get into this? You two look like you're having so much fun. I wish I could find something . . ." In each instance identical words were said with the same envious inflection. As we talked with these women who were searching for something to do, we also met more and more who had found their "thing," and were happily working at it, paid and unpaid. We began to formulate a vague idea for a new book.

The new year came and with it another luncheon invitation

from our publisher. It had practically become an annual affair by now. This time when he asked what we had in mind for our third cookbook, we gave him some suggestions we had worked up and as an afterthought, we mentioned our idea concerning women "doing something." We were not particularly articulate in our presentation, and it was not discussed at length. A week after our meeting, very much to our amazement, we received a phone call from our publisher. "Drop everything girls and get to work on 'women.' We like the outline, see what you can do . . ."

We were completely nonplused—for a moment at least—before we decided to proceed in our customary plunge-ahead fashion. We both, after all, were a part of the story of women which gave us experience from which to write. Nevertheless, the current avalanche of popular literature on the subject had completely passed over our heads. We decided the obvious first step was to go to the library and find out who we were historically, sociologically, and culturally.

Chapter *II*

From Then To N. O. W.

*F*or most of us the Women's Liberation Movement has seemed too loud, too aggressive, too sensational. The stridency of the movement has turned us aside from listening to the sincerity and credibility of its demands. Since we didn't want to be identified with its style, many of us became alienated from its content. Involved with home and family, we have understandably felt detached from the battles for equal job opportunities, child care centers, and non-discriminatory laws. Above and beyond the obvious benefits of laws which they have forced through recalcitrant legislatures, we have all been affected to some extent by the agitation of our more militant sisters. As they have demanded and received equal recognition in the marketplace, all of us can't help but have an improved sense of what a woman can do, if she wants to.

Ann Reed and Marilyn Pfaltz are cookbook authors and

lecturers. We both know from our own experiences that self-confidence is not only the key to success but is absolutely essential to the first step taken in any direction beyond the safety of home and family. There have been proliferating studies, surveys, and articles exploring woman's curious lack of self-confidence when she is faced with situations beyond her domestic domain. It takes the same courage to say "no" to an insistent salesman or to return a piece of moldy meat to the grocer as it takes to apply for a job, start a business, or write a cookbook.

A woman's reluctance to project a positive image outside the family is part of her cultural inheritance of being female, of being thought of as the "second sex" since the beginning of recorded time. To read the history of women from Eve to N. O. W. is to understand how greatly we are affected by the traditions and actions of all the generations that came before.

According to the anthropologists, nomadic woman of ancient time naturally assumed the tasks of gardening and homemaking while her husband was out hunting food with stone and club. She was bound to the campfire by monthly cycle and reproductive function. Bearing children was uncontrolled and for centuries quite mysterious. In this age of hunting and scavenging, woman enjoyed a brief span of time as a Supernatural Being. Her ability to bring forth children was as awe-inspiring as was the earth's capacity to germinate and nurture crops. She was entrusted with matters of the soil, partly in hopes that her godlike powers might help the vegetables. Woman, as Earth Mother, was half-feared and half-worshiped by man as the strange source of the land's regenerative power.

The discovery of tools to subdue the soil expanded man's understanding of the growing process. He was no longer dependent on the caprices of nature. He learned about planting, irrigation, and harvesting. As he enlarged his garden patch into a field, woman's strength became unequal to the heavier tasks of cultivation. Man actively and aggressively shaped his own destiny by conquering his environment. He made the earth produce at his direction and the animals submit to his desires for food, clothing, and harnessable energy. Woman, made passive by her dependence on man's strength and by enslavement to the reproductive process, repetitiously pursued the chores of daily survival. As man's knowledge progressed, the magic of woman's power began to fade.

Society gradually changed from a nomadic to an agricultural one. In order to increase production with added strength, man enslaved his fellowmen to work the land and relegated woman to the hearth. Land became property. Life began to have a past which was last year's crops and a future which was next year's yield. Children assumed a value not only as extra field hands but as a means to continue ownership of property.

Turning his back on the superstitions of an earlier age, man seized control of his life. He became master, owner, and supreme family authority. Woman took on the important but nevertheless secondary role of nurse and servant, while man possessed and directed the authority of society. Prevailing thought held that man's body produced the seed of life and woman's function was to nourish. For that reason man took the privilege of handing down these rights to his male descendants. In our cultural heritage patriarchy became a firmly entrenched historical fact at least five thousand years ago and has remained virtually unshaken ever since.

As society evolved man and woman were thrust into mutually exclusive roles. The separate lives ordained for men and women may be analyzed in their political, legal, social, commercial, and sexual spheres.

Politically, man was ruler of family and nation. He was explorer and conqueror. Government was for men only, except for the rare instances of an occasional queen who was projected into power through a temporary chink in the male armor. As institutions of government developed, women were excluded by law and practice from participating as officials or voting members of the community.

Legally, woman was considered property, in most cases valued property, but nevertheless part of a man's estate. With few transitory exceptions from the days of Hammurabi to Blackstone she has been assigned the same legal status as minors and incompetents.

Socially, woman has been more or less segregated from male company since the beginning of civilization. Men have justified protecting their wives from the company of other men, supposedly in fear of allowing women to become too worldly. As a result women have been gathered or assembled into harems, temples, and convents and hidden themselves behind their own veils, sewing circles, and women's groups.

Commercially, most occupations were male prerogatives. Woman's admitted lack of superior strength and mobility during childbearing and childrearing years forced her to take on the household chores. She readily assumed the role of helpmate to man's professions.

Sexually, from the anthropological origins of family living to the space age, custom has insisted upon a woman's premarital chastity and marital fidelity. Within the marriage relationship, woman has been expected to play her part in a non-aggressive, modest, and virtuous manner. Traditionally, the passions characteristic of wanton temptresses were not appropriate at home.

Thus, recorded history began with man firmly established as head of the household. The classical civilizations of Egypt, Mesopotamia, Palestine, and Rome created a status for women through tradition and law. With some variation and few exceptions this status has remained unmodified for three thou-

sand years. Even modern European man, who felt compelled
to change and improve his cultural inheritance from these
ancient civilizations in the areas of art, science, law, and
religion, never thought to reevaluate the conditions under
which women existed. Woman's status was considered fit and
proper according to inherited patriarchal traditions, customs,
and values. Politically, legally, socially, commercially, and
sexually, woman played a role that was pre-ordained and un-
alterable in the minds of men.

The biblical beginnings of woman were inauspicious to say
the least. After God had created man in His image and assigned him dominion over every "living thing that moveth
upon the earth," God said that it was not good for man to be
alone. He would make a companion for him, so Eve was taken
from Adam's rib. Eve has always been blamed for their fall
from grace because of the apple tasting, but it should not be
forgotten that Adam presumably bit into the fruit of his own
free will, tempted or not. God's wrath is legendary, and the
banishment from Eden is well known. Also remembered is
God's angry curse upon Eve, directing that her desires be
subject to her husband who shall rule over her from that moment forth. Thus spake the Old Testament!

The legal position of a Jewish woman was little different than
her predecessors or counterparts. As was common practice, she
was disallowed inheritance, and upon her husband's death
became dependent upon the charity of her sons. She was
assigned a special screened section of the synagogue for wor-
ship for fear her charms would distract. Girls were generally
not sent to school but were taught the necessities of the household arts at home. However, suppressed as she was both legally and socially, the Jewish woman was greatly honored in
her marriage by a devoted husband. He was bound to monog-
amy by religion and marital fidelity by tradition. As mother
and wife, she occupied a position of the greatest importance to

the family's welfare. As the Proverbs describe, she was a house-keeper without compare: "She seeketh wool and flax and worketh willingly with her hands . . . she planteth a vine-yard . . . she layeth her hands to the spindle and her hands hold the distaff . . . she maketh fine linens and selleth it; and delivers the girdles into the merchant . . . she looketh well to the ways of her household, and eateth not the bread of idle-ness. Her children arise up and call her blessed; her husband also and he praiseth her."

The ordinary Grecian woman of early antiquity was bound to home by law and by society. Legally she remained a per-petual minor, under the guardianship of either her father, her husband, or the state. She was unable to make contracts, bring legal actions, or inherit property. She spent most of her life in the gynaeceum or women's quarters to the rear of the house. She was only allowed out infrequently to visit friends and relatives and to attend special religious celebrations. Harlotry was the only profession which allowed women to escape the seclusion of the family compound.

A large number from the Greek lower classes took up resi-dence in brothels or in temples supported by "religious" prosti-tution. A number of higher class women sought escape as en-tertainers at all-male affairs where they performed much like a Japanese geisha. A very select group called the hetaerae were especially cultured and educated to become mistresses to the great men of their day. These "companions" preferred un-licensed unions to marriage which was restrictive and did not allow their participation in cultural or political affairs.

The status of women at the height of the Classic Age of Greece was described by Demosthenes: "We have hetaerae for the pleasure of the spirit, concubines for the daily health of our bodies, and wives to bear us lawful offspring and be faithful guardians of our homes."

The Roman Empire evolved a much greater social liberty

for women. They were not secluded in special quarters within the home but were allowed to be seen in the streets and attend theatres and athletic games. As mistress and mother, she was in charge of the slaves and directed the education of her children. She was regarded as a companion to her husband and shared much of the domestic management. She was respected and valued for her maternity. Prostitution was legally restricted in Rome and was generally clandestine in practice. For lack of opportunity, marital infidelity was uncommon. The family unit was a recognizable strength of the State, and the Roman matron appeared very much a liberated woman, as compared with her Eastern sisters.

Free as these ladies were to oversee a household and move about in public, for purposes of law they were referred to as "imbecilitas sexus." No matter how worldly the women of Rome became they were still under the yoke of legal subjection. Cato impassionately expressed the point of view of at least one element of Roman society: "If we had, each of us, upheld the rights and authority of the husband in our own household, we should not today have this trouble with our women. If you now permit them to put themselves on an equality with their husbands, do you imagine that you will be able to bear them? From the moment that they become your equals they will become your masters."

The Age of Antiquity which had seen the magnificence of Egypt, Greece, and Rome, was brought to an end by barbaric invasions, resulting in general poverty and chaos. A rise of Christian temporal power heralded the beginning of the Middle Ages. Disillusioned by the events of history, man abandoned his belief in knowledge as power, and power as right, and immersed himself in the credo of faith, hope, and charity. The utopian wish of medieval man was to attain God's infinite goodness and mercy. The Church became omnipotent as the final arbiter of God's will and incidentally of woman's status.

Canon law decreed marriage to be a sacrament and adultery a sin. A wife was required to obey her husband and he was obliged to protect and support her. St. Paul defined the position of woman without beating around the bush: "Man is the image and glory of God but woman is the glory of man." Paul went on to describe woman's role: "Wives, submit yourselves unto your husbands, as unto the Lord. For the husband is the head of the wife, even as Christ is the head of the Church." However, the potential power of woman's charms did not go unnoticed by the Church, and celibacy was officially imposed on the priesthood.

The medieval peasant woman worked as hard in the fields as her ancient nomadic ancestor. Times were tough. Famine and plague, war and peace, came and went with relentless regularity. A popular theme in medieval folk literature was the clash between a husband's brutishness and his wife's superior guile. This everlasting struggle produced probably more sexual equality than any law decreed.

Wives of feudal lords were no less busy than their peasant counterparts, but the work was physically less trying. As the household manager of an estate, she oversaw the kitchen, bakery, and laundry. She superintended the brewing of beer, preserving of meat, and making of clothing. When her husband went to war, she was expected to assume total responsibility for the operation of the land and castle. Man's business was to fight, hunt, feast, and make love. However, according to custom, romantic love was not thought to be found in marriage. It was argued that marriage combined a maximum of opportunity with a minimum of temptation. Knights dedicated battles and pledged undying devotion to another lady worshiped from afar by poem and letter.

Medieval Christendom was for woman the best of times and the worst of times. It was the age of the monk and the age of the knight. It was the epoch of Mary's divinity and the epoch of sensuality. It was the season of chivalry and the season of barbarism. Woman was wooed in rhyming couplets by knights errant and beaten for trivial transgressions by domineering husbands. Church and civil law severely inhibited her legal action but custom and tradition allowed her extraordinary freedom.

During the Renaissance, rigid Church morality was gradually replaced with an overwhelming devotion to esthetics. Art, architecture, music, dance, fashion, conversation—all flourished. Concern for the life hereafter was subordinated to a wild pursuit of happiness on earth. The hard times of the previous centuries slowly gave way to wealth and luxury. For a woman of rank it was the best of times. She was finally permitted to attend the universities and became a charming and educated part of the intellectual life carried on in courts and in salons of the privileged.

With the unveiling of her mind, came the disrobing of her body. In fashion, she was barebreasted, adorned in robes of silk and velvet, much rouged and bejewelled. In art, painters worshiped her nude charms and outdid each other in capturing every tone of her flesh on canvas. Politically, Catherine de Medici, Isabella, and Elizabeth were reigning examples of what a woman could do if given half a throne or more. The Renaissance woman of charm and beauty, of fashion and intellect, was to the manor born.

Her peasant sister was still hard at work in the fields, uneducated and completely dependent upon her husband's protection and support. Her life was inextricably bound to the seasons of sowing and reaping. The major turning point in her strenuous existence was the rise of commerce and industry as a way of life to replace an agricultural economy. Gradually a middle class developed to become the manufacturers and merchants. Invention of the loom and the printing press produced new trades. The guilds often included women who were skilled in the new professions of weaving and silver making. Education for women was no longer a luxury but an economic advantage.

The Catholic Church which had developed from the simple teachings of Peter and Paul to the all-powerful governor of citizen and state alike began to lose its grip. The final authority of the Pope was challenged repeatedly by new monarchs ascending their thrones. The universal power of the Church was broken by the Protestant Reformation led by a German monk, Martin Luther. An immediate radical change was permission for the Protestant clergy to marry. A sizable number of young women had been educated within convent walls, and the widespread dissolution of monastic orders created a need for elementary schooling for both male and female.

Luther, following his own dictates, married an ex-nun. His views on woman's place are worth noting here since he did speak for a movement and as a husband with a large household of six children. Perhaps his thoughts should be read remembering the German tradition of "kinder, küche, and kirche"— a belief that woman was divinely designed for childbearing, cooking, and praying. Luther is quoted as saying, "Take women from their housewifery, and they are good for nothing. . . . If women get tired and die of bearing, there is no harm in that; let them die as long as they bear; they are made for that."

The family unit gradually replaced the Church as the hub of life. Renewed emphasis on the Ten Commandments produced strict public morality, and the growth of a prosperous bourgeoisie stimulated a decline of private morality. The Teutonic view of a patriarchal society influenced every household, moving one historian to observe, "Women were goddesses before marriage and servants ever afterwards." Within the home she was mistress of much but in the political and commercial world she was master of nothing.

The momentous discovery of a new land across the ocean opened the eyes of Europe to the prospects of gold and the possibilities of land acquisition. Most of the early settlers who came to North America were not escaping from political oppression or seeking religious freedom. They were hoping for an opportunity to own land and start a new life in an unexplored world which beckoned with undiscovered riches. The importance of women during these first years of settlement is poetically described by a planter from the original Jamestown Colony just prior to the arrival of the first shipment of "tobacco brides" from England: "When the plantation grows to strength then is time to plant with women as well as with men; that the plantation may spread into generations. . . ."

The second wave of arrivals in the new world were seeking political freedoms as well as land. Eventually persecuted Quakers, Puritans, Separatists, Catholics, Dutch Calvinists, and others joined the original colonists and set up varying forms of government in towns scattered up and down the Eastern coast of America. The beginning of colonization was a hard-fought battle to survive against the forces of nature and the increasing unfriendliness of Indians angered by the takeover of their lands. Women were equal partners in this struggle, needed as much for their strength as for their childbearing and domestic talents.

Although there were many religious sects that settled in New England, the majority were Puritans, and their strict style dominated the early history of the region. The pulpit was greatly concerned with the conduct or misconduct of woman. She was continually reminded that it was Eve, one of her own kind, who had tempted Adam into wickedness. As a descendant of the first sinner on earth, she should spend her life striving for holiness of spirit. Her penance was a lifetime mission of doing good works. Piety, modesty, and chastity were the virtues of a reputable woman. Puritan names such as Comfort, Faith, Mercy, Prudence, Patience, Charity, and Submit revealed the demeanor expected of her.

To judge from the preachings of a stern and sanctified ministry, the lives of Puritan ladies should have been quite restrictive and extremely chaste. Actually, society permitted not only the custom of bundling but quite practically allowed a pre-contract or in more modern words, a trial marriage. The Seventh Commandment forbid adultery, not pre-marital sex! On the other hand, dancing was considered the Devil's delight and a threat to morality.

The fundamentals of reading, writing, and simple sums were taught to women that they might better study the bible, help tend a husband's store, and keep accounts. Often she was forced to take over for a spouse or father and run his ship or business. It was not unusual to have woman butchers, tanners, barbers, shoemakers, and gunsmiths.

There were no provisions, legal or otherwise, for women to participate in colonial politics. None of the eighteen women aboard the *Mayflower* was asked to sign the Compact which history records as the first document of representational government in America. In Puritan New England a woman had a tough enough job tending to her virtue that she needn't meddle in the affairs of state.

The continuous thread which unravels from the creation of Eve and weaves through the pages of history is that equal freedom and opportunities in society have never been granted to women by law. From time to time individual women have held positions of influence and power. Married women have most always been protected or cared for under the laws of property. However, no matter how little or great was her freedom according to custom, under law she could do very little. Her life was legally confined to perpetuate woman's role as defined by preceding generations.

These same generations had also established a feudal society of privileged and non-privileged classes. Until the eighteenth century, society had categorized people by reason of birth, religion, and sex, and they held jobs accordingly. Land and wealth were concentrated in the hands of a privileged few. Political and religious institutions had become corrupt. More and more there was talk of man's inalienable rights—liberty, equality, and justice for all. People wanted the right to do what they wanted, not what their father and grandfathers had done before them. A new class of merchants, wholesalers, shopkeepers, and guild-masters resented the inequalities of society and began to agitate for reforms. Both the French and Americans held successful revolutions to overthrow undesirable tyranny.

John Adams, well known as a libertarian, together with Thomas Jefferson had been selected to draw up a Declaration of Independence for the colonies. The following excerpt from Abigail Adams' letter to her husband and his reply serves as a clear indication where matters stood in 1776 as regards women and "equality." Abigail wrote:

. . . In the new code of laws which I suppose it will be necessary for you to make, I desire you would remember the ladies and be more generous and favorable to them than your ancestors. Do not put such unlimited power in the hands of the husbands. Remember all men would be tyrants if they could. If particular care and attention is not paid to the ladies, we are determined to foment a rebellion, and will not hold ourselves bound by any laws in which we have no voice of representation.

That your sex are naturally tyrannical is a truth so thoroughly established as to admit of no dispute. But such of you as wish to be happy willingly give up the harsh title of master for the more tender and endearing one of friend. Why, then, not put it out of the power of the vicious and lawless to use us with cruelty and indignity with impunity? . . .

John replied:

. . . . As to your extraordinary code of laws, I can not even laugh. We have been told that our struggle has loosened the bonds of government everywhere; that children and apprentices were disobedient; that schools and colleges were grown turbulent; that Indians slighted their guardians, and negroes grew insolent to their masters. But your letter was the first intimation that another tribe more numerous and powerful than all the rest were grown discontented.

Depend upon it, we know better than to repeal our masculine systems. Although they are in full force, you know that they are little more than theory. We dare not exert our power in full latitude. We are obliged to go softly, and in practice, you know we are the subjects. We have only the name of masters, and rather than give this up, which would completely subject us to the despotism of the petticoat, I hope George Washington and all his brave heroes would fight; I am sure every good politician would plot, as long as he would, against despotism, empire, monarchy, aristocracy, oligarchy, or ochlocracy. . . .

The founders of this new republic proposed that the best government "is one in which the laws are made and administered by elected officials popularly chosen for their intellectual and moral superiority." Women were not included in this democracy as either electors or the elected. Abigail Adams' letter reflected the views of a growing number of women who were displeased at being excluded from the new liberties being offered to men.

In 1792 Mary Wollstonecraft in England wrote a much publicized book entitled *Vindication of the Rights of Women*. In it she attacked the prevailing view that women were the weaker sex, superior in charm and grace to men but inferior in wit and intellect. Her book passionately advocated equality between women and men. She wrote, "The first object of laudable ambition is to obtain a character as a human being, regardless of the distinction of sex. . . . Marriage will never be held sacred till women by being brought up with men, are prepared to be their companions rather than their mistresses." Her private life read like a Dickensian novel, and it was no wonder she railed against the tyranny of men. She had grown up with a drunkard for a father and lived with several men who were more than casual in their regard for her affections. Her book was to become the Magna Charta of the first stirrings among rights-conscious women that resulted in a full-blown feminist movement.

Woman's "century of struggle" began in the early 1800's. Prior to then names, dates, and places have been relatively unimportant to this general historical narrative describing the status of women. However, from the beginning of the nineteenth century there is a recognizable feminist movement gathering momentum. Names and dates are a convenient way to follow its progress. It is startling to realize how close so many of the significant events of the movement are to our own or parents' and grandparents' memory.

In the early days of the nineteenth century American women were mainly concerned with the good works of their church. They had begun to form their own organizations for discussion and for charity work among the poor. There were many causes which attracted their attention, but the determination of the abolitionists to grant slaves their human rights struck a responsive chord in women's hearts. In the first half of the nineteenth century Lucretia Mott, an educated and eloquent speaker in the Quaker ministry, became a luminous spirit in organizing the first anti-slavery groups. Soon to become good friends and fellow workers in the cause were Sarah and Angelina Grimke. The Grimke sisters were born to wealth and luxury in the South, and from their early experiences and observations soon became fervently opposed to the practices of human slavery. They moved North and became Quakers in order to dedicate their lives to their convictions. They pioneered a speaking tour, lecturing on the liberation of the slave as much as on the responsibilities of women to free themselves from their traditional and confining status. They wanted women to "make use of religious and literary privileges and advantages within reach, if they will only stretch out their hands and possess them." In order to become a part of the great moral reformation of the day, women must stop worrying about "the bounds of propriety, which separate male and female duties and inquire only 'Lord, what wilt thou have us to do?' "

Sarah and Angelina Grimke passionately believed that women should become involved in politics, "inasmuch as we are citizens of this Republic and as such our honor, happiness and well-being are bound up in its politics, government and laws." They were cruelly attacked in press and pulpit alike for their inflammatory speeches.

Thankful as the abolition movement was to receive women's support for its cause, its male members did not allow ladies to sit on committees nor sign any public declarations and proclamations. As more and more distaff abolitionists became angered by arbitrary restrictions which limited their actions, the cause of women's rights began to gather steam. The last straw occurred in 1840 at a world anti-slavery convention held in London. Lucretia Mott and Elizabeth Cady Stanton (another prominent name in the fight to free the slaves), together with about a dozen other women, traveled three thousand miles to attend. They were refused admittance because of their sex, and were placed in a balcony behind a screen from which they could hear but not participate in the convention's proceedings.

These enraged women returned to the United States determined to take action. Eight years passed before Elizabeth Stanton, then living in Seneca Falls, New York, persuaded Lucretia Mott to join her in calling a convention to publicize these views.

The Seneca Falls Convention in 1848 has been generally acknowledged as the official beginning of the Women's Rights Movement in America. Both men and women attended. The main contribution of the convention was the passage of a "Declaration of Sentiments" which enumerated the specific grievances that women held against society. The Seneca Falls Declaration listed those rights which were unavailable to women and discussed at length abuses suffered because of the attitudes which men had assumed about women. It concluded on a note of challenge:

> Now in view of this entire disfranchisement of one-half the people of this country, in view of the unjust laws above mentioned, and because women do feel themselves aggrieved, oppressed, and fraudulently deprived of their most sacred rights we insist that they have immediate admission to all the rights and privileges which belong to them as citizens of the United States.

Whether or not the Declaration was completely founded in fact, the truthfulness of its overall argument made a significant public impact. Most newsworthy was a demand for the vote. This was the first public expression in favor of women's suffrage and had been inserted by Elizabeth Stanton over the protests of some of the more conservative delegates.

Eventually the suffrage struggle was to become the guiding motive of the women's movement, and it was unceasingly fought for the next seventy-two years with the help of both men and women.

Following the success of the gathering at Seneca Falls, one

convention led to another as a means of propagandizing the sentiments of the movement. New names and faces joined the active lists. Susan B. Anthony from New York rapidly became the genius at organizing and coordinating the movement's efforts. It was an uphill struggle. As these intrepid women traveled from city to city pleading the cause of human rights, they continually encountered apathy among their own sex. The immodesty of the feminists, who appeared and spoke in public, and the irreverence of their disturbing thoughts, turned many women against the movement. The majority of housewives were little concerned with thoughts or aspirations beyond their domestic realm. Limitations on their legal and political rights seldom affected them directly, or so it seemed. It was frustrating for a reformer to be told by a lady with a husband and six sons, "I control seven votes, why should I desire to cast one myself?"

Many of the feminists came from privileged circumstances and were not overly concerned with the plight of their poorer sisters. They were more inclined to expend their oratorical energies on matters of voting, holding elective office, joining the professions, and being able to enter the better colleges. This was pretty heady stuff for the ordinary nineteenth-century woman. Susan B. Anthony, however, emphasized better economic opportunities for women, that is to say—jobs. Working concerns had a wide and immediate appeal to the average woman.

The Civil War halted reform activities, and the ladies threw themselves into the war effort. Many of them risked their lives nursing the dying and wounded. They held great fairs to raise money for military hospitals. Others replaced men who bore arms by taking over the jobs left behind. Julia Ward Howe composed the "Battle Hymn of the Republic." Clara Barton organized a volunteer nurse corps. Harriet Beecher Stowe wrote *Uncle Tom's Cabin*. In spite of invaluable services performed during wartime and years of devotion to the cause of abolition, women's equal rights and vote were not included in the fourteenth and fifteenth amendments which conferred citizenship and the vote on Negro men.

It was a bitter disappointment. Feminists determinedly gathered their strength and resumed the battle for women's suffrage. However, their ranks were in considerable disarray. An ideological split developed within the movement. Moreover, an infamous affair involving one of its prominent members and the notorious antics and scandalous speeches of some leaders had managed to get the whole cause identified with free love. Confusion and scandal as well as the movement's growing fixation on the single issue of suffrage lost many supporters of the original cause for women's rights.

Nevertheless, as the century prepared to turn, attitudes concerning women had reluctantly begun to change. The myth of physical frailty and delicate sensibilities was being laid to rest by the extraordinary stamina of body and spirit exhibited by the lectureresses on the suffragette circuit. With unruffled calm these women braved primitive travel conditions, hostile audiences, and an abusive press. Belief in her mental inferiority was being disproved by ever-increasing numbers of graduates from a half dozen women's colleges and co-educational institutions available to her. A handful of women were making their way into professions despite many obstacles. Elizabeth Blackwell applied to twenty-nine medical schools before finding one which would accept her. As the first woman doctor she went on to found the New York Woman's Infirmary Medical School. There was a growing demand for nurses and teachers, and the invention of the typewriter opened new opportunities for women in business.

The condition of women was being altered by other inventions such as the iron range (1840), the sewing machine (1846), kitchen sink (1880), commercial cleaners, canned goods, and other prepared foods. Children were now in school for longer hours in the day and for more years. Improved medical care made women feel healthier and more energetic. Sports such as tennis, swimming, and bicycling were very much in vogue. Contraceptive information was at least available, although still an unmentionable subject. Advocates of birth control as well as marriage reform and free love shamelessly preached their messages from the podium. This was hardly a sexual revolution, but Victorian prudity was under attack.

Politically, there were some encouraging developments. Several of the Western states had granted women the vote. Other states had intermittently allowed women to cast ballots in school board or municipal elections. Still others had revised their property laws and were considering a review of divorce, inheritance, and other related legislation.

Although not yet an emancipated woman by today's standards, by 1900 she had come a long way. She was brighter and stronger, and she was ready, willing, and able to reform the world.

The influx of European immigrants to industrialized America had overcrowded its cities, and new problems arose to claim the attentions of reforming spirits. Women took on the causes of education, prisons, care for the insane, prostitution, foreign heathen, factory working conditions, and most importantly—temperance. "Purity in the American home" was their battle cry. Women by the hundreds of thousands joined the Women's Christian Temperance Union calling on liquor dealers to "place yourselves in the ranks of those who are striving to elevate and ennoble themselves and their fellow men . . . in the name of our desolate homes, blasted hopes, ruined lives, widowed hearts, for the honor of our community, for our happiness, for the good name of our town, in the name of God who will judge you and us, for the sake of our own souls which are to be saved or lost."

For the first time an organization had attracted women from all segments of society and all sections of the country. The temperance experience was producing a phenomenon peculiar to America—a volunteer brigade to serve as a social conscience. The whole country was breaking into women's clubs by town, state, and nation. As more women became involved, support for the suffrage movement revived.

In 1907 Elizabeth Cady Stanton's daughter returned to America from a twenty-year stay in England where she had been involved in the English feminist movement. She brought with her an entirely new and militant style. Pickets, protest parades, and hunger strikes replaced the lectures and petitions of the first generation of feminists. The question was no longer if, but when the suffrage bill, known as the "Anthony Amendment," would pass.

However, prohibition beat suffrage by a single year. In the wake of reforming zeal which accompanied America's entry into World War I, national prohibition was signed into law as the eighteenth amendment in 1919. A strange alliance of interests coalesced to prevent women from voting: powerful liquor interests who equated suffrage with temperance; the urban political machines, which feared an uncontrolled political constituency; southern politicians who did not want an additional black electorate; and a sizable number of conservatives who felt it was unnecessary to rock the status quo.

The National American Woman Suffrage Association rallied to the challenge and mounted a vigorous campaign from state to state. On August 26, 1920, Mrs. Carrie Chapman Catt, head of the Association, traveled to the Tennessee legislative session where the final vote for the states' ratification of the nineteenth amendment was cast. It was seventy-two years after the "Declaration of Sentiments" from Seneca Falls. Mrs. Catt later summarized the efforts: "52 years of campaigning; 56 state referenda campaigns; 480 drives to get state legislatures to submit suffrage amendments to votes; 317 campaigns to get state and national party conventions to include suffrage planks; and 19 campaigns for the 19th Amendment with 19 Congresses."

Yet the vote so highly prized and so dearly won did not radically change women's status. Just as legal prohibition failed to cure the social ills caused by alcoholic intemperance, suffrage did not overcome three thousand years of tradition and attitude. Somewhere in the 1890's the original cause for a general reform of women's rights to establish her equality in the business and social worlds and to reevaluate her legal position in family and society was obscured by an obsession to obtain the vote. The battle was won but the victory soon became empty.

The disenchantment which set in following the nineteenth amendment is described in a social science journal of 1929: "The true concept of woman is of a being with a mind, with *specific* talents which need to be developed *and used;* . . . until this principle is accepted as ultimate as shaping not only education, but social forms, we shall look in vain for progress." With the apparent victory of suffrage, feminism faded as an issue in American politics not to reappear again until 1961 when President Kennedy established the Commission on the Status of Women.

Nonetheless, decade by decade during the intervening years, as manners and morals of society changed, so did the status of women. The flapper of the Roaring Twenties became a symbol of the new, uninhibited moral code. Freudian theory brought out an awareness of sexual attitudes. It was a popular theory to embrace, and the invention of the automobile encouraged its practice, as did the startling frankness of movies and confession magazines. Social and sexual freedom carried over into the business world. As married women and girls from well-to-do families sought jobs previously held only by women "who had to work," women found a new sense of independence.

The depression of the Thirties brought an abrupt end to the flamboyance of the previous decade. Traditional upper- and middle-class attitudes toward working women gave way when her income was needed to put food on the family table. A working wife became socially acceptable when the alternative was public relief.

The advent of World War II in the Forties brought thousands of women into wartime work to replace men in military service. Rosie the Riveter was a product of modern technology. Women could no longer be considered inferior because of their lack of strength. They drove trucks, flew airplanes, and repaired engines. Women joined the armed forces and went into combat as nurses, correspondents, and photographers. However, when the war ended, returning servicemen resented competing with women for the jobs they had left behind. The natural reaction for women was to return home and start having more babies than ever before.

Magazines, movies, television, and books of the Fifties idealized the role of wife and mother. Freud's theories were revived to explain women's role, "anatomy is destiny." Dr. Spock, whose book was the young mother's bible, knowingly declared, "biologically and temperamentally, I believe, women were made to be concerned first and foremost with child care, husband care and home care. . . ." One notable statement in dissent against the picture of domestic bliss was made by Simone de Beauvoir. Her book *The Second Sex* received critical intellectual acclaim as an eloquent, literate declaration of women's status.

The Sixties propitiously began with President Kennedy's

official recognition of "women" by his establishment of the President's Commission on the Status of Women. Then, in 1963, Betty Friedan wrote *The Feminine Mystique,* which verbalized and popularized the thoughts and feelings of millions of tradition-bound housewives. More militant sisters in small but visible numbers surfaced as political activists in both the peace movement and the civil rights cause. Public attention was focused on legal inequities and discriminatory practices against women by the report of the President's Commission. Congress and state legislatures reluctantly began to cope with inequalities. The Equal Pay Act (1963) and Title VII of the Civil Rights Act (1964) banning sex discrimination in employment were legislative milestones more in theory than in practice. The lack of enforcement for these laws is what compelled Betty Friedan and others to form the National Organization for Women (N.O.W.), an action group dedicated to achieving full equality for women. This decade saw the awakening of women's consciousness.

In 1972 the Equal Rights Amendment to the United States Constitution was finally passed by Congress, fifty-one years after it was first proposed. "Equality of rights under the law shall not be abridged by the United States or by any States on account of sex." State by state, legal ratification is slowly becoming a reality.

For women, the Seventies is the best of times. Medicine has given us extra years and extraordinary health. Technology has given us the gift of time. Feminists have won for us the protection of law. Society has offered us the opportunity to fulfill our potential beyond the role of wife and mother. For each of us, the destiny of our lives is more in our hands than ever before.

Chapter III

Rediscovering "I"

*I*f the natives of New Guinea could read English, do you suppose they would recognize themselves as the same people described by anthropological jargon in the *National Geographic Magazine?* They would probably be surprised to discover that they are "acting out societal roles" and "conforming to behavior patterns" as they go about their primitive businesses. Most of us feel the same surprise when we recognize ourselves as part of the history of women. Unaccustomed as we are to considering ourselves a part of anything but our family, it comes as a bit of a shock to understand that the subject heading "women" is us.

Most of us have been generally oblivious to feminist stirrings of the past or the present. Nevertheless it is difficult to avoid recognizing the new emancipation of women. Medical and technological developments, equal rights legislation, a gradual change in public attitude plus an increasing need for extra income to provide the luxuries we have always enjoyed are all major factors which have produced today's working woman. There is a certain inevitability in statistics which can be disturbing if we are not planning to become one of the three out of five marriages that ends in divorce or in this case one of the four out of ten married women who enters the work force.

Society has historically expected very little from women outside of their natural destiny as wife and mother. Everything has been so much of a pattern—college, marriage, children, a few hobbies mixed in with community activities, and then retirement. There has been little opportunity and less inclination to break out of this mold, so solidly cast by the habits of previous generations. Feminist agitations in the Sixties finally precipitated changes in law and custom which have produced the choices and freedom of the Seventies. Freud or no Freud, the anatomy of today's woman is her destiny for a far shorter time than ever before.

The new challenge facing us all is what to do with twenty extra years, give or take a few. These are the years after children no longer need full devotion and attention, years after a noticeable reduction in family responsibilities, years which begin with the thunderous silence of an empty house.

Each of us becomes aware of this silence at different times in our lives. For some, it is the day the baby of the family goes off to kindergarten for half a day. For others, it occurs when the youngest child leaves for college. As with so many significant stages in life, realization of change comes as a delayed reaction to events. A trivial incident so often is the spark which illuminates the full sense of what has happened.

"When my youngest went off to school I was so involved with volunteer activities that I hardly noticed her absence. I had no plans to occupy the new-found hours other than to do errands and attend meetings without worrying what to do with Sarah. It was several busy years later that I was struck as if by a thunderbolt with the realization of just how many free hours I had or could have if I wanted them. This flash of understanding came one morning as I indulged myself by watching the movie *Love Story* on television. As I sat there with a cup of coffee in one hand and a handkerchief in the other enjoying a good cry, it suddenly hit me. My children were all in school! I could go to work if I could find a job."

The shock of empty hours comes gradually and differently to every woman. Less than a generation ago, the years after children left home and before retirement seemed too few for a woman to become involved seriously with any new endeavor. These years were a period of gradual disengagement, a general drifting in anticipation of the close of a husband's career. Feelings of restlessness and vague desires for recognition were dismissed by society as merely expressions of personal problems. Betty Friedan's book *The Feminine Mystique* was responsible for revealing these frustrations to be symptomatic of a woman's desire to seek an identity in addition to her role of wife and mother. Subsequently, journalists, scholars, and broadcasters alike have taken up the cause of liberating woman from her traditional entrapment in a full-time homemaking career. There is a great deal of pressure from the media to conform to the current popularized image of the modern emancipated woman "fulfilling her potential."

Her "twenty extra years" challenges today's woman to add a new dimension to her life. The opportunities are exciting and limitless whether or not she stays home, volunteers, or takes on a paid job. The problem with being handed an opportunity is that it forces us to make choices, of accepting or rejecting the challenge, of doing something or doing nothing, of developing or retiring.

The emotional whirlpool most of us go through when we

come to this crossroads in our lives is illustrated by one woman's description of her experience with an unexpected highway interchange. "One night I was on my way into the city to meet my husband for dinner. It was just dusk as I entered the stream of cars hurrying toward the bright city lights which were beginning to come on across the river. Sweeping around a bend in the road I suddenly encountered a large cloverleaf intersection which I had seen under construction for several years. Now it was completed and all traffic was being routed through it. There were at least four turnings that I could take, and from a distance they appeared not to be well marked. I was seized with unreasoning panic as I felt pressed by the drivers behind me to choose my course without knowing where I was going. If I took the wrong road, I would not only be lost but be horribly late for dinner. At the time, I wasn't sure which prospect was worse, careening along on a super highway interchange at fifty-five miles an hour toward heaven knows where or anticipating the wrath and worry of my waiting husband. Completely undone by both thoughts, I swerved out of the traffic on to a small dirt construction road to collect my wits. Eventually I figured out my course and made my way into the city on time."

A woman's "twenty extra years" is much like the cloverleaf on that highway. We've known for a long time that it was coming, but it is not until we suddenly come upon it that we must cope with it. If we don't pull over to the side of the road and decide which turning to take, the traffic will sweep us on to wherever it is going.

"Where am I going?" is a question which has no easy answer. "I" is no longer a singular pronoun. Once upon a time making a decision involved me, myself, and I. Now "I" concerns my husband, my children, my car pool, my committee meeting, my tennis game—all of the involvements and commitments assumed through the years. The horizons of a woman's life begin at the altar to narrow into an extremely self-contained world of family and friends. Overnight "my" life becomes "our" life. Many busy years go by before there is free time and energy left over to take more than a passing interest in the world beyond the view from the kitchen window.

An amusing summation of "then to now" by a forty-ish contemporary hits an exposed nerve. . . . "Unaccustomed as I was to being a cook, housekeeper, launderess, paramour, handywoman, and worldly companion, the first romantic years of marriage as advertised were more blissful in memory than in practice. Unfortunately college had ill-prepared me for my new geisha existence and I worked hard those first wedded years adjusting to my new career. I had barely adapted myself to being the multi-purposed bride when I found myself with child. I don't mean to imply we didn't discuss having a family, but somehow the enormity of what we had begun didn't occur to me until I donned my first maternity outfit. I was immediately welcomed into the hitherto mysterious sorority of motherhood by friends and strangers alike, all anxious to share their personal experiences. Once again I had a new job for which I was singularly unskilled. I soon discovered the myth of maternal instinct was of little help in coping with midnight colic and toilet training.

"However, the physical exhaustion brought on by the 'tote and carry' stage of early child-rearing was nothing compared to the additional mental fatigue of school years. Adolescence was an emotional shock to the family's collective nervous system from which recovery takes time. Meanwhile my mornings were spent on a volunteer merry-go-round, and afternoons were consumed by chauffering anybody everywhere. Days slid into years. My children learned to drive, and I stopped saying 'yes.' Unexpectedly my precious free time became empty hours. It took a while to realize the job of motherhood was over. Now what . . . ?"

This is a common storyline to most of our lives although events and personalities shape the differences. Some of us lead narrower lives than others and become totally submerged in activities and desires which immediately touch or affect our family and community. Some of us participate more than others in pursuit of politics, social service, or education. But all of us are bound by the real or imagined demands of our marriage contract. Spurred on by the media, we attempt the impossible role of being all things to all people. Our identity is absorbed into the lives of those who live in our world. We become somebody's wife, so and so's mother, good friend, helpful neighbor, and concerned citizen.

As we acquire each new role we also assume real and imagined responsibilities. Our real duties are practical and obviously go with the job. The imagined responsibilities are better described as expectations. They are each woman's image of herself as wife or mother or whomever, as well as the image she thinks everyone expects her to portray. When carried to an extreme, these expectations become psychological blocks which affect our actions. It is no wonder that "we" drifts further and further away from "me."

Facing the real life crossroads of fulfilling a second lifetime startles most of us into self-encounter. Before deciding "where am I going?" it is necessary to know who "I" is, to understand what the singular "I" really wants and needs. The moment of truth comes when we start peeling off the layers of responsibilities, expectations, hang-ups, and images which we have acquired through the years. It is impossible to turn back the clock completely and find the eager college student or innocent young bride. Too many experiences have been accumulated over the years to find either one. Even so, there is a "me," who isn't somebody's anybody, hidden beneath all the encumbrances natural to a woman's life. It is "me" who must choose what I could, would, or should do with my twenty extra years.

Instead of driving blindly ahead through life's cloverleaf and risk being carried off to an undesirable destination, most of us should pull over and come to grips with *where, who,* and *why.* The first step is to understand what is real or imagined. How many things have we done in our lives because we thought we should. We must face our own behavior and recognize what is essential to our various roles and what is unimportant.

Traditionally, boys played with trucks and planes and girls played with dolls. Boys grew up to be doctors, lawyers, and Indian chiefs. Girls grew up to be mothers. A young man had an infinite variety of choices to explore in selecting his career. A young woman had an inevitable destiny—marriage—and her simple choice was to whom. Fortunately for society most of us wanted to do what we had to do. Those were the years that were. We, who have been married for ten years or more at this reading, belong to those traditions.

It is highly unlikely that many of us ever sat down with our prospective husbands and worked out a contract of rights and duties or a settlement of career conflicts. Instead it was mutually understood and expected that a wife's responsibilities were to give moral support to her husband in the pursuit of his profession. Her fulfillment and status were to be derived from his achievements and from her satisfactions in having and raising children. She was to give her husband love and encouragement to go forth in the world, while she became creator and keeper of the family life-style at home.

"Little did I realize when I promised to love, honor, and obey that implicit in the bargain was hand-ironed shirts and a full-course breakfast daily." Everyone has their own style!

The relationship of wife to husband which relies so greatly on silent communication and personal interaction is difficult to describe in generalities. In the beginning there is a commitment based on shared emotions and physical need. As time passes a pattern of giving and receiving is established.

"The morning I arose and remembered it was the last day of the month to have the car inspected was the beginning of 'one of those days.' Since the car had been my assignment, I really did not care to bring up my delinquency at breakfast when we were all discussing the upcoming day. Those mornings when I want to leave the house earliest are always the days both Jim and the children seem to go into slow motion. It is agony to watch them all looking for notebooks, briefcases, packed lunches, brushing hair, and finding gym clothes, when I am all ready to fly through the door. With an absentminded kiss on the cheek, Jim left saying, 'Have a good day and be sure to get my blue suit from the cleaners. I need it tomorrow.' Thank goodness, he had forgotten about the car.

"Until everyone had left, I had not dared to look in my calendar. My worst fears were more than confirmed when I saw what I was supposed to do that day clearly written in pen. Getting the car inspected was going to be the apple that toppled the cart. Not counting the dishes, beds, and waiting laundry, the first thing I had forgotten I had to do was drive a carload of fourth graders across town to a puppet show. Unfortunately the performance would not be long enough to allow me to drive to the inspection station and back. Poised in mid flight between the kitchen sink and the beds, I couldn't decide whether it would take longer to get a substitute driver or go myself. When the first phone try drew a busy signal, I recognized the handwriting on the wall and flew back to straightening things.

"This was also the day I had a long-standing appointment to have lunch with a convalescing friend, and I couldn't bring myself to disappoint her at this late date. The question was should I try for car inspection after the puppet show and before lunch or after lunch and before the kids got home from school? The latter course seemed the least hectic. I called my friend to explain I would be earlier than originally planned, if she didn't mind.

"Twelve noon found me back from the fourth grade excursion but without the proper papers for inspection which I had left back at the house. Haste has always made waste ever since I first started hurrying, but I've never learned my lesson. Rushing to be on time for my early lunch date, I fumbled at the door and managed to allow the dog to escape. I didn't know whether to have hysterics on the stoop or take up the chase through the backyards in hopes of catching him before he disappeared completely. 'Come' has never been a command our dog obeyed, and he wasn't going to change his habits now. With the help of a passing stranger, I finally captured the runaway and banished him to his bed. I was now only a half an hour late!

"Lunch was delightful but brief. Alternately apologizing and explaining, I hurried us through lunch and rudely left after two sips of coffee. When I arrived at the state inspection station I was relieved to find only a few cars ahead of me. I had just enough time to pass through and be home for the children's arrival from school, or so I thought. Unbelievably the car didn't pass. All I could think of was that Jim will kill me when he discovers I waited until the last day and then failed. Seeing my ashen face, the inspector helpfully suggested that the nearby service station could probably adjust the headlights while I waited. Fighting down a rising sense of panic, I roared off to the garage. As the mechanic tinkered with the lights, I was able to call a neighbor to ask if she wouldn't mind putting a note on the door for my children, telling them I would be back momentarily and not to go away.

"The inspector was awaiting my return, and I am not sure whether it was properly adjusted headlights or my visibly agitated behavior which caused him to stick his official seal on the windshield. At least I arrived home before the rioting had begun on the doorstep. However, I was greeted with 'Mother, Mother, where have you been? I promised you would drive the car pool this afternoon. Mrs. Kroll is sick and you said you would be home.' Somehow the day was going absolutely out of my control. I decided not even to waste a breath in protest since I could do my grocery shopping between trips.

"Luckily, the week before I had made a delicious lasagne which was waiting in our freezer for just such an emergency. Dinner miraculously was served more or less at the usual hour, and my adventures at the inspection station amused everyone. The evening's events were yet to be coped with. As it turned out Jim had a town board meeting which I had forgotten. I hinted that perhaps none of us needed to show up at the PTA meeting at school. The children's reactions made me realize one of us was indeed expected to appear and that I'd better hurry up before I was late. Fortunately our oldest can take sitting charge, and with a minimum of bedtime and homework instructions Jim and I left in separate directions.

"I sat exhausted in a half hypnotic state throughout most of the PTA meeting, mentally retracing the day. Suddenly I had a stab of memory. Dear God! I had forgotten Jim's blue suit at the cleaners. My poor tired brain snapped to attention as I tried to figure out what he was going to wear instead. The rest of the meeting seemed to pass very quickly. Arriving home in an absolute fit, I found Jim and the children happily watching television together, bedtimes and homework forgotten. Much to my relief his green suit would do just as well for tomorrow's meeting.

"Finally the children were in bed, the last dish was put away, and everyone's outfits requested for tomorrow were rescued from the laundry. The late movie's theme song was just coming on when the television was turned off, and in answer to Jim's question, I was not too tired. . . ."

Unquestionably motherhood is one of the most important jobs in society. Ironically it is the one job which does not demand previous experience or even prior knowledge. There is no required training, and there is little on-the-job supervision. Arriving home from the hospital with a new baby is a proud and frightening moment. It is one of life's miracles that babies survive the trial-by-error ministrations of their young mothers.

The fear of not knowing how to handle a baby is overcome with practice and considerable reliance on Doctor Spock's book. The real apprehension comes from reading the comments of psychologists concerning early child development. Magazine articles point out that a child's life pattern is formed at very early ages. Heaven forbid that a life pattern should develop from those early years of constant confusion when a busy husband is pursuing his new career and an inexperienced mother is running after toddlers. Most of us never take a course on raising children. Reading about sibling rivalry, stifling creativity, and image building only increases doubts that we know what we are doing. Fathers are equally anxious, but since they are generally at work when crises arise such as who hit whom and who should be spanked, the burden of developing the child naturally falls on mother.

A mother invests a great deal of time and patience in training preschool children, and the test of her abilities is when they finally enter school. Are they polite? Do they share? Are there any bad habits?

A wonderful first teacher experience was told by a friend. "I really couldn't believe Sally, my first baby, was actually going to school. But in early spring a notification had arrived requesting mother and daughter to have a get-acquainted interview with the kindergarten teacher. As we approached the school my heart was pounding with pride and excitement to show off my first child. Sally was a reluctant debutante as much from extreme shyness as from a terrible cold in the head. I had to pull her along as we walked down the corridor. The teacher was very charming. Throughout the interview Sally sucked on her finger as she tried to breathe through a stuffed nose. As we got ready to leave, the teacher turned to her papers, pencil poised, and said with teacher-like enthusiasm, 'I see Sally is a fingersucker. We will certainly do something about that!' I could have died. I blushed from inner fury and frustration but had the wits not to protest. In truth Sally had never sucked a finger in her life, but I realized it was no moment to explain about colds. . . .''

Most of us can't help but feel that teachers think our children's behavior reflects our training. From the moment our children enter school our job as a mother is vulnerable to public comment. Paradoxically, we try to develop each child's sense of independence and individuality, but at the same time feel somehow personally responsible for their grades and actions. We attempt the impossible task of pleasing family, school, society, and the child. According to tradition mother stays home and brings up the family. Professionals warn that her physical presence is the key to emotional health. Neighbors are quick to explain that the problems with the children down the street is that "the mother works." Children pathetically ask if you are going to be home after school, so that they may have a friend in. It is no surprise to find women have been reluctant to fly in the face of forecasted doom. Unless it was an economic necessity to go to work, mothers have generally stayed home while the children were small. Interesting careers were either abandoned, interrupted, or never begun.

The measure of a mother's achievement is her success in

raising children who will happily leave home without needing her. It is a strange career which creates its own end. The loss of the job is inevitable, yet there is seldom any thought of unemployment or plan for job retaining.

A woman develops a living pattern for herself and family almost unconsciously as she carries out the responsibilities of wife and mother. Since most of us have no advance preparation for managing a home and family nor probably have given it any thought, circumstances and the media guide our original actions. We fall into a way of doing things which at first is a matter of habit and then frequently becomes a question of ritual, for better or worse. How often we respond to a child's plaintive question "why do I have to" with the irrefutable answer "because, that's why!"

House and Garden perfection, as portrayed on television and in magazines, sets impossible standards in all areas of homemaking. Today's woman is envisioned as a gourmet cook, innovative decorator, entertaining hostess, talented needle-worker, and accomplished gardener. It is difficult to resist society's pressures to achieve some kind of reputation for something. Since there are no promotions or salary increases for the homemaker in her professional world, public recognition such as "she bakes her own bread" or "she makes all her clothes" becomes her measure of success. Somewhere along the years we have to choose what is worth our commitment.

A mother of four children and assorted pets describes her self-revelation as a housekeeper. "When I was a young expectant mother in a small apartment, I spent hours dusting, polishing, reading, and teaching myself to cook. I took pride in my immaculate and shining home. Fifteen years later, I had become a constant nag trying to keep my house in the manner to which I had become accustomed. One afternoon I overheard a conversation between my son and his friend deciding at whose house to play. 'Let's go to my house, it's more fun,' said the friend. 'Your mother is always complaining about the mess we make.' "

We all realize sooner or later that housework expands to fill the time allotted for it. For some of us it is a labor of love. For others it is a challenge to overcome with dispatch in order to make time for our own pursuits at home, in the community, or in the professional world.

A friend who has taken on a part-time job describes a shopping experience. "I flew into a nearby supermarket one morning before being even later to work than usual. The aisles were crowded with clusters of chattering women. Recklessly I pushed my cart through the store on a dead run with one eye on the shelves and the other on the clock. I was breathless when I arrived at the checkout counter only to find one machine in operation and a long line of women patiently waiting their turns. I could hardly contain myself from screaming at such obvious inefficiency during busy hours. As I tried to calculate just how late I was going to be, I overheard two women in line talking about the difficulty of shopping at this store because the manager never gets around to opening the other registers. Says one to the other, 'Oh, well you have to pass your time somewhere I guess.' That did it. I pushed my bulging cart to one side and left."

It is very difficult to sort out the real motivations for accepting the first volunteer jobs. In the early years of baby tending, a young mother feels utterly housebound. Since she is inexperienced at the job, there is a period of adjustment before she finds the time to do anything but diapers and bottles.

"I can still remember the first year with my first child as being the busiest time in my life," said a mother of four. "My angel daughter slept in snatches, and I took care of my small apartment in snatches. The minute she went down for a nap

I would quickly put in a load of laundry, fix a sandwich, and sit down happily with a good book. I never seemed to read more than a few pages, but she was up again. I was always exhausted from nervous tension, anticipating her every cry and squeal. There is nothing like several years of on-the-job training with three more babies to transform a nervous young mother into the assertive captain of a pre-school troop. Looking back I can't imagine how one small baby could have taken so much time. When the phone rang asking me to serve on a hospitality committee at church, I leapt at the opportunity to have a legitimate reason to get a babysitter and go out into adult company."

A woman's first volunteer jobs are most often serving on committees that provide refreshments or make phone calls. The beginning jobs are social and give a volunteer an opportunity to meet others in the community and learn how people and things function. It also gives the volunteer establishment a chance to size up the newcomer. As in business there is a definite volunteer ladder of success. The second rung is a committee chairmanship. This position is offered to those who establish a reputation of being able to get things done. It is a promotion in recognition of achievement. The volunteer receives the self-satisfaction of being appreciated for her effort and ability.

Once discovered as a willing and capable worker, her phone never stops ringing. The woman who builds a reputation of efficiency and effectiveness begins her ascent to the top of the volunteer ladder. She serves as a board member, on the executive committee, takes on special projects, and eventually has an opportunity to become president. Along the way she can experiment with her capabilities. Unlike the professional world, the volunteer arena offers many training experiences. She can discover her own level of abilities and decide whether

she is better suited as a leader or a follower. Community involvement fulfills her need to feel useful through serving
others.

All too frequently most of us become overcommitted. It is
flattering to be asked to perform a task, and it is satisfying to
take charge and do it. It is difficult to say "no" to friends who
ask for our time, and there is always a thought that too many
refusals will remove us from the social stream. Children's and
husband's activities often direct our volunteer interests. We
are frequently propelled by circumstances and fail to recognize these years as a work experience which could be leading
us anywhere. A disturbing sense of fragmentation accompanies
the volunteer role. There may well be public recognition for
time invested, but true personal satisfaction is elusive. It is
difficult to pursue any activity in depth. Unpaid personnel are
not regarded as professional. There is a feeling of being a
jack-of-all-trades but master of none.

"It seems strange to sit in a meeting . . . listening to all
the business of the organization . . . feeling absolutely removed . . . not disinterested, but rather amazed with my lack
of adrenalin spurts as each new point is brought up. Two years
ago I was totally immersed in the policy making thoughts behind the talk of this morning. Since then, I seemed to have
faded out . . . most of what goes on has gone on before,
same proposals but new people making them. I guess I am
ready to retire . . . I truly feel I don't need the companionship . . . I have done so many of the jobs . . . I am thankful
for the confidence I gained in doing them . . . I don't need
to direct, manage or lead any more. I understand the necessity
of the motions but I can't believe they matter much . . . at
least to me . . . besides there are many young new faces as
I look around . . . also yesterday was my fortieth birthday."

So much of what a woman is concerns her being everyone
but herself, of being an image created by the existence of

others. All our married life we make decisions according to the needs and demands of others. There is no opportunity to make our own choices. What to do with twenty extra years is a choice. What does "I" need for those years?

We need to be accepted for ourselves and not as a "collection of functions." We need to feel the impact of our own individuality. We want personally to experience a proof of contact with life—a sense of having an effect. We need more than our husband's position and our children's accomplishments. Our own identity has been obscured by the multiplicity of roles to which we have adapted and adjusted our lives. We need a single-minded purpose of our very own.

Chapter *IV*

Second Choices

*T*he opportunities for a woman in the 1970's to "fulfill a second lifetime" are greater than they have been before. Everyone is concerned that she be busy, happy, and productive. So much of what we do is directed by events and the pressures of our people-relationships. Decisions in a woman's life usually are the result of a combination of circumstances rather than a consciously prescribed plan. It can be very unsettling to come face to face with the realization that there really is a chance to "do something" of our very own. Such a confrontation means making choices which most of us have had little practice in doing. The anticipation of changing a comfortable, relatively secure living pattern is exciting but disturbing. The unknown is always a risk.

Throughout history a woman's place has been well defined by law and custom. Her attitudes and actions have been ordained by the expectations and restrictions of society. Protected first by her mother and father and then by her husband, she has been living in a domestic cocoon safe from the judgments and evaluations of a competitive world. For a woman to venture beyond the emotional and financial security of her household cloister takes a great deal of self-confidence. It takes courage to expose herself to public view and submit to being measured by standards other than her family's.

Confidence level and financial need are two factors which most affect our selecting a course of action or non-action. It would seem that the need for money should be the major consideration for women going into the marketplace. Obviously if a family requires additional income either for necessities or luxuries, mother can go to work. Unfortunately, mother is probably "out of touch, out of training and out of demand" with the business world. More important in finding a job, she is out of confidence.

There is a mystique to the working world which is awesome and imposing when viewed from the sheltered life most of us lead. Everyone "out there" seems to have a skill or talent which is recognizable. After all, they are being paid for it. This aura of achievement is intimidating. What have we been doing at home all these years? Whatever it is, it is surely hard to define. An ability to cope with the demands of a husband, children, friends, neighbors, and a community is not readily acknowledged as a marketable talent. Our mental powers have been occupied with important but unworldly problems in daily family living—should the boys get haircuts, does it really hurt their feet to pass down shoes, what will we do this vacation? "Out of touch" is the understatement of the year!

The result of trying to serve so many masters is a kind of fragmentation of body and soul. We are continually asked to be here and there, to do this and that, and to answer "yes" or "no." We are consulted as an authority on all manner of unfamiliar subjects. The smattering of knowledge we accumulate over the years is more frustrating than satisfying. The rewards of a well-run house and a loving family are intangible at best. There are no promotions, and the salary is spent on food and clothes. Love and appreciation are unmeasurable. Confidence founded on such illusory accomplishments is a fragile thing. Most of us can be quite assertive publicly on behalf of our family. It is when we have to make our own way that our self-assurance wavers. For so many years our minds have been committed to family use that it almost takes a physical effort to shift our attentions from them to me. Nothing is a greater boost to the ego than acquiring a skill or mastering a subject.

"My mother is always amused when I give her a tour of my latest garden acquisition. She still vividly remembers Saturdays trying to get me to weed her garden before I rushed off to some high school doing. One of her favorite stories from those days concerned her asking me to dust the roses. As she tells it, she came around the corner to find me carefully wiping each petal with a cloth. She completely despaired at my ignorance and disinterest in growing things.

"It is difficult to remember exactly when the horticulture scene caught my interest. My first challenge came when we moved into our present house, and I tried to maintain the gardens in a manner to which they had become accustomed. I never knew so few flowers could take so much time. I was determined to keep them alive. Reluctantly, I had to admit I began to enjoy their care. A knowledgeable friend, realizing my struggles with life and death in the garden, took pity and became my mentor. Her enthusiasm was contagious. In spite of kickball, football, and baseball, the flowers bloomed, and I only lost a few bushes to the winter sled runs. As the children grew older, it became safer to expand our plantings. I attended some lectures and even took several courses. Not knowing of my past rose-dusting days, the local garden club invited me to become a member—an honor in which my mother took a great deal of vicarious pleasure.

"Soon other people began to ask my advice on garden matters, and I experienced the satisfaction of having mastered something. I extricated myself from non-gardening extracurricular activities which had begun to consume my days. I accepted only volunteer jobs I enjoyed, from beautification projects to running the plant booth at a YWCA Christmas fair. Working in a neighbor's greenhouse preparing her cuttings is where I found my calling. I loved the smell of damp moist air and the feel of potting soil. I desperately wanted my own greenhouse. Up to this time my husband had been most indulgent of my garden extravagancies and took pleasure in their results. Putting a costly addition on the house in order that I might putter around in dirt was a different matter. My success with the YWCA plant booth, and everyone telling him how I had coaxed all kinds of rare and sickly seedlings to flourish must have convinced him that a greenhouse was my destiny. Christmas morning I was presented with a very large package which contained a very small poem.

> Imagine a wife who wakes up and sings,
> She deserves a few green growing things.
> If potting and rooting such happiness brings,
> A greenhouse is yours from all your darlings.

"I was completely surprised and delighted although I couldn't help but protest the expense. 'Never mind,' my Santa Claus said, 'we've got two years before Jane needs college tuition. Who knows, maybe by then you'll be supporting us all from the sale of exotic plants.'"

Public recognition for a personal accomplishment is the beginning of a "raised consciousness," to use the current vernacular. As a new community member and a young mother, volunteering is at first a social outlet. When the children become less dependent and are less at home, we are apt to find ourselves more involved in organizational workings. Then is the time to ask the question, "Why am I doing this?" So many of us get on the volunteer treadmill without thought or direction. Often we are carried along into jobs for which we have neither the time, talent, nor inclination. It is very hard to say "no" to a friend. An honest self-appraisal of our motivations for taking volunteer opportunities gives a purposefulness to saying "yes" or "no." Understanding what "I" can do, want to do, and have time to do builds self-confidence from which to plan a volunteer career and avoid the frustration of a fragmented life.

"I was a math major in college for no other reason than because I was good with figures. Marriage to Stu saved me from a long job hunt. My four years of calculus and advanced mathematical theorems were reduced to balancing the family checkbook. Somehow my college career leaked out, and I was persuaded to become the treasurer of an organization which I had joined ostensibly to become more involved politically. Once a treasurer always a treasurer is a volunteer maxim! Over a period of years I served as treasurer for all kinds of groups, activities, and projects. I enjoyed a reputation as the local 'keeper of the books,' and I was learning a great deal about business and finance along the way. However, though much of this kind of work is done at home, the various board meetings requiring my attendance seemed to fall always on the one night I was needed for a family crisis at home.

"Out of the clear blue I was approached to be treasurer of a brand new 'Show and Sale' venture being undertaken by the hospital auxiliary. It was to be a three-year commitment and would involve setting up my own bookkeeping procedures. My first reaction was, 'You've got to be kidding. You need a professional accountant!' The very persuasive hospital director assured me they could only afford a volunteer such as myself.

"That evening my husband and I had a long after-dinner chat concerning how much accounting did I know and how much could I learn in a hurry. Stu's reaction was for me to take the job and worry about the double-entry details later. 'If you don't take the job, they will get someone else just as unprofessional. After all, they certainly won't fire you. What do you have to lose?'

"The answer was, 'a great deal.' Stu was an advertising copy editor who stayed as far away from figures as possible, and it was all very well for him to advise. I almost believed the myth of my enviable understanding of financial figures. However, self-confidence was a fleeting thing, and did I really want to lay it all on the line? Three years was a long time, but I could look forward to finally putting all my eggs in one basket. I would have a good excuse to resign from everything else. I could sign up for an accounting course at a nearby community college which would be a means of reassurance for my faltering confidence. With Stu's blessing and much soul searching, I took the challenge and said, 'yes.'

"Looking back over these years as my term of office draws to a close, I am aware of how much this job has changed my life. My children have been impressed with me going back to school and proud that I can manage 'all those ledgers.' Unbidden, they have willingly taken on all kinds of responsibilities which I had been trying to get them to do for years (such as dishes, beds, leaves, etc.). I have had to sit in on meetings with the hospital's staff members, and I find that they are impresed by the 'Show and Sale' and are surprised by the healthy income which it generates.

"The obvious question which floats through my mind is, what next? I could spend the next two or three years and become an honest-to-god accountant. I have just a few short years left before all three children are in college, and my time will be virtually my own. On the other hand I selfishly cherish the independence of volunteering, of not being tied down to a 9–5 job, of possibly traveling with Stu on his frequent business trips. Fortunately, I still have six months to think before I 'retire.' Wishfully, by then volunteer hours will be equated to the minimum wage scale. Even now federal legislation is being proposed to allow a volunteer to take a charitable deduction for hours given. With luck I could become a tax deduction!"

Volunteering has been a way of life for American women since those first ladies rolled up their sleeves to care for the dying and wounded on the Civil War battlefields. Historically, women have dedicated themselves to humanitarian causes and services. Abolition, prohibition, child labor legislation, civil rights, suffrage, prison reform, equal rights . . . have all responded to the impact of women's support. Over the years women have harnessed their collective energies and altruistic impulses into leagues, clubs, and groups of all description. The volunteer hours contributed by these service organizations are the backbone of our healthy communities. Social agencies have become dependent on their unpaid staffs to function effectively. As a volunteer typist, receptionist, bookkeeper, fund-raiser, administrator, organizer, or runner of things and errands, we are in great demand.

A volunteer career has a variety of obvious advantages. There is freedom to come and go. The restrictions of daily office routine are minimal. There are opportunities to sample different types of jobs, to discover what is enjoyable and suitable. A volunteer job may offer a greater possibility of finding a position of significant responsibility than as a paid employee. Often there is less anxiety connected with an unpaid job because there is no competition among employees for salaries, commissions, and bonuses. If the job doesn't work out it is

acceptable to beg off for "personal reasons." Such a resigna-
tion is not as readily identified as failure in the volunteer
world as it is in business.

The main concern for most of us is maintaining our family's
equilibrium. Women are unaccustomed to functioning as independent individuals in public. Subconsciously we tend to seek
responsibilities which are merely extensions of our homemaking tasks. Traditionally a woman plays a dependent role
within the home. A successful involvement with outside activities changes her status just enough so that everyone, husband and children alike, must pause and adjust their image of
Mother. There's a delicate balance between a man's world
and a woman's place. Most of us are reluctant to rock the boat
if the captain is looking seasick.

"As an art major in college I looked forward to working in
textile design or a related field. For two years after graduation
I had a fascinating job with a fabric house. I was thrilled to
get married but sad to move away from my job. We rented a
very small apartment in Boston where Peter's company had
sent us, and I learned to cook. The first months were fun and
different, but frankly after a while I was bored with an entire
day to do as I pleased. My suggestions for getting a job fell on
deaf ears, and looking back I think Peter was relieved to find
I was pregnant at last. I think it was a source of pride to him
that I didn't have to work. So many of our friends had to start
out with two salaries. Three children arrived in rapid succes-
sion, and the tempo of our lives was caught up in daily main-
tenance and frequent business transfers. Peter's career was
very much on the rise, which made the many moves bearable.
During those years I looked at a lot of houses.

"Overnight the children were in junior and senior high
school. I had spent years on and off PTA boards and various
educational art committees. I needed a change of scene. I be-

gan to look around to see what I might do. A chance remark made everything fall into place. I had agreed to help with a benefit house tour and serve as a hostess in one of the homes. As I stood in the living room pointing out the particular items of decorative interest, a friend in the assembled group laughingly spoke up, 'Hey, we aren't here to buy the house. You've missed your calling. Come to work at our real estate office.' I took her seriously and appeared in her office the next morning. She explained the licensing procedure which involved taking a course and passing state exams.

"That night at dinner when I eagerly told Peter of my new found opportunity he was less than enthusiastic. He felt it would take too much time away from the family. He was sure I would exhaust myself trying to keep up my standards of housekeeping perfection. After many days of persuasion, he agreed that I could at least take the course to see if I really wanted to pursue the idea. Not only did I manage the course with a minimum of family life disruption, but I passed the state boards with flying colors. I was ready, willing, and eager to go to work.

"It was then late fall and Peter felt I should wait until after Christmas when all our visiting relatives had come and gone. The real estate office agreed to expect me by January. All December I ran around the house straightening drawers and closets, thinking it would be a long time until I would be able to do that again. In passing, Peter commented about the possibility of my going on a business trip with him as well as some business entertaining he needed to do after the holidays. The moment of truth was precipitated by a phone call from the mayor asking me to serve an appointive five-year term on the Board of Education. As flattered as I was, I was prepared to refuse since the real estate office awaited my imminent arrival with baited breath, I hoped. I truly wanted to be a professional. I needed the satisfaction, which I well remembered from my early working days, of being paid for something I was trained to do.

"I was completely taken aback when Peter advised me to accept the mayor's appointment. I recognized then that the handwriting had been on the wall for months, but I had failed to see it or perhaps didn't want to look. I had ignored all of Peter's hints along the way assuming that the details could be worked out. Unfortunately I wasn't listening to his need to be the sole provider for the family at this stage in his career. Confidence is a fragile thing for all of us. The implications of my going to work were upsetting to Peter. I realized that his image of the successful executive did not include a working wife. Part of his ambition and drive was his desire to succeed for me and the children. As an unpaid member of the Board of Education I would not disturb his sense of purpose. He was proud that I was asked to serve the community in such a responsible job, as time-consuming as it would be. How could I refuse? Perhaps in a few years when Peter's career is more settled another job will come along. . . ."

As the economic pressures of this decade mount, economists have turned their attentions to women and their potential impact on the job market. We seem to be a highly significant labor statistic which everyone is studying and evaluating. Demands of an ever tightening economy, expanding educational and career opportunities, and desire for more than reflected glory from a husband's career or a child's academic progress have brought women to the brink of the marketplace. To work or not to work, is the choice facing today's women.

Fear of failure is a major stumbling block to taking a job. Contemplation of emerging from the secure and familiar confines of a woman's place into the aggressive, competitive dictates of an unfamiliar professional world is nerve wracking. The stigma which for generations society has imposed on the working wife and mother is difficult to overcome. It takes a reservoir of confidence and determination for a mother, especially with young children, to begin or resume a career. She must wrestle with her own conscience about the quality and quantity of time devoted to her family. She must be able to resist guilt feelings brought on by critical neighbors and her inability to be always home. And most importantly, she is responsible for her family's adjustment to her new schedule as well as to her new image. For some households this adjustment means a mutually agreed upon division of labors. For others it means mother gets up earlier, works faster, and goes to bed later to be sure her employment doesn't interfere with expected family routine. Lifestyle is a personal thing.

"I was happily settled in the suburban swing of PTA meetings, car pools, and a weekly tennis game. Singing had always been my great interest. In college I sang in the chapel choir and concert chorus as well as singing the leads in musical shows. I loved doing all three, but my favorite was concert work. I was used to the hierarchy for church soloists, and, as a newcomer, I patiently served my apprenticeship in my church. I began taking voice lessons again from a fellow choir member who happened to be a voice teacher as well as the musical director of a nearby Masterwork Chorale. Eventually I did quite a bit of solo work for the church including a guest spot or two with other choirs. The congregations were always very kind, and my singing received many compliments, which was great for the ego.

"My teacher was demanding more and more from me, and it was exhilarating to hear my own voice respond to his coaching. One day he greeted me with a paying offer to sing the contralto part in a Shubert piece the Chorale was performing. I was overcome with stage fright even at the thought. I wasn't nearly good enough. He insisted I was as good as any singer he had ever hired, which may have been pride of instructorship. He admitted my inexperience but tried to persuade me that it was a perfect opportunity to begin professionally. I must admit such dreams of glory had fleetingly occurred to me. Somehow the idea of being paid made me feel very insecure. It was one thing to be a big fish in the church musical circles, but it was quite another to be accepted as a professional soloist by a highly competent and critical choral group. Without ever mentioning it to Jim at home, I indicated I didn't feel ready for the job. Besides there would probably be too many rehearsals for me to attend. As luck would have it Jim and the director ran into each other the next Sunday and had a lengthy discussion of my abortive career.

"Coming home in the car, Jim was amazed that I hadn't leapt at the opportunity. 'You've always said you wanted to turn professional. What's the matter with you now?' My protests about rehearsals and babysitting were brushed aside with generous offers of his help. I had run out of reasons for saying 'no.' Fortunately the part was still unfilled, and the director was very pleased to have me change my mind. I cannot logically explain the difference in nervous strain which accompanied my paid performance and the dozens and dozens of unpaid solo appearances I had made over the years. Part of it was coming face to face with the reality of a fantasy. Sometimes it is just easier not to risk failure and loss of a dream."

The need for extra income in support of either necessities or desirable luxuries is an unquestionable imperative for seeking a job. An ambition to achieve in the business world, for whatever reasons or however limited, is a radical departure from the expected financial and emotional dependency of being a housewife. It takes a while to get used to making decisions which do not involve checking with all members of the family. It is difficult for most of us to emancipate the mind and spirit as well as the body from being wife and mother. A large measure of independence comes with financial self-sufficiency.

"I had arrived at college wanting to major in art in order to do portraits. Ever since I could remember I scribbled on a sketch pad. Faces held an irresistible fascination. Just to please a friend I joined a class in sculpture and fell in love with clay. Trying to capture a face from the unshapen gray lump was a far greater challenge for me than painting. Graduation came too soon for most of us. I emerged ill-prepared for the commercial world, after being pampered and protected in the academic scene. Bounding around Europe, studying, seemed a good way to put off trying to find the inevitable teaching job. I spent days sitting at a table in an outdoor cafe on the Boulevard St. Germaine passionately arguing away the hours. Eventually good sense, family pressure, and lack of funds (not necessarily in that order) compelled me to stop 'studying' and come home.

"I secured a teaching job at a private school which was located in a university town. In no time at all I discovered a group of artists who steered me to a sculpture class which I managed to squeeze into my teaching schedule. I was thirty-one years old and beginning a new career. Marriage was the farthest thing from my mind! Then I met an attractive doctor who swept away all my protests about settling down. In a few short years, I had become a not so young matron with two small children as well as an extremely frustrated sculptress trying to find time and space to work. I finally abandoned even trying which, I guess, in the end was less upsetting. I threw myself into all the activities that go with raising children in a suburban community. Ted was busy building his medical practice, and thirteen years escaped me before I felt free enough to join the local art center.

"I was so out of touch with the whole scene that I signed up for a pottery course. I felt less exposed to the harshness of artistic judgment working in a craft. Somewhere along the line I brought home some clay and, working in the corner of the dining room, did a head of both children. They were good. I had not completely lost my touch. A friend spent weeks trying to persuade me to do one of her child. When I agreed, I found myself unexpectedly catapulted into a career. One commission began to lead to another and I realized I had to have a studio.

"When I broached the subject to Ted, planning to work out the cost, unthinkingly he said, 'Sure, get the builder and figure out something in the basement. Don't worry about the price. It's great that you keep so busy.'

"He was astounded at my explosion. I was furious to be considered my husband's indulgence. I told him angrily that I fully intended to pay for every penny of the addition from my own earnings. When my temper cooled I realized that Ted's attitude was partially my own fault. I'd been working in and around everyone's schedule so as not to disturb either Ted or the children. Since I wasn't making any demands, no one in the family took my work very seriously. Ted was wrapped up in his practice, and he was unaware of my growing professional acceptance. Fury aside, I truly wanted the satisfaction of knowing my work paid its own way. It was a point of pride and independence not to be under any obligation even to my well-meaning husband."

Money begets status in our economically oriented society. It is the undeniable measure of success, as much as we would like to think better of ourselves. To the world in which we live, pay means recognition. The worth of an accomplishment is judged more by the money it receives than by the praise it deserves. The income and prestige of the marketplace cannot help but beckon us all.

The traditional tempo of a woman's life is changing. Society is encouraging a natural evolutionary process. We can more gracefully experience marriage, motherhood, homemaking, volunteering, and taking a job without making the peremptory choices of "either-or" along the way. Each role has its time and place in our lives.

"My culinary career began with a YWCA cooking class on breads. Up until then cooking had been a pleasant chore, something I did because we had to eat. I had come a long way from my early married days of looking up a recipe for baked potatoes. As I learned about yeasts and doughs and the history of breadmaking, I caught a sense of the creative art of food preparation and realized what a fascinating subject it was. I seemed to have some time in my life, and I was looking for the stimulation of reading and learning something new. I found a great satisfaction in mastering soufflées and meringues. Needless to say, Ed and the children enjoyed my experimentations, and they encouraged me with their enthusiasm. Now when an organization wanted a casserole I took pride in producing the most unusual and the most delicious. I began seriously gathering recipes and cookbooks and organizing the collection. In the back of my mind was a vague thought of someday doing something with all my clippings and cards, although I didn't know what. I must say it made entertaining more difficult, since I no longer could just throw some things together. I had to maintain my newly acquired reputation of being a gourmet cook.

"When the children finally were all in school all day, a friend and I enrolled in one of the big-name cooking schools. Surprisingly it was not much more professional or informative than the several courses I had been taking at the YWCA. A half-formed notion floated through my head that I could give a course as well myself. For the moment, to my regret, I was very involved with several volunteer organizations. I had already run my shares of dinners and dances, and I didn't need to serve on any more committees. I jumped at the chance to head the gourmet booth at the annual church fair and have an excuse to back off gracefully from some of my other commitments. I was anxious to try out some of my ideas about creative cookery. I stuck my neck out and planned some different and unusual menus. The proceeds of the booth would be an obvious measure of success or failure. Modestly I must report we made the biggest sale ever recorded. Thank goodness!

"After the fair, as I was casting about in my mind looking for a new challenge, I received an unexpected phone call. A nearby adult school was desperate for a replacement instructor in its cooking course. Without hesitation, I said yes. The details of the school's schedule versus my routine would just have to work out. I didn't even know what the cooking subject was. It was immensely flattering to be considered a professional, and this gave me confidence to take on whatever was planned. When I told Ed what I had agreed to do, without a moment's hesitation or thought, his comment was, 'Well, at last you are going to get paid for all your efforts.' The nicest thing about the entire experience was my unexpected financial windfall, small as it was. I had wanted to recover our living room couch but couldn't seem to justify the expense. With my proudly earned lecture fees, I grandly sent it off to the upholsterers.

"I loved teaching the cooking course, and I found that I probably related better to the ordinary housewife than a high-powered professional lecturer trained at the Cordon Bleu. The enthusiastic response of my class turned me into an expert practically overnight, much to Ed's amusement. He still remembered my humble kitchen beginnings. With his blessing I embarked on a full-time part-time career as a cooking school instructor for the YWCA's adult schools in the surrounding towns.

"Fortunately I could do all the research and testing at home. The children were impressed that I was being paid to tell people how to cook. Since I made a superhuman effort not to disrupt anybody's routine and juggled all my commitments around the family's needs, everyone was thrilled with my 'work.' I got used to doing household chores on a dead run and laundry in every spare minute. There was a new emphatic ring to my voice when I said 'no' to the calls asking me to bake or drive or whatever. I more or less faded out of the organizations to which I had belonged. I am ever grateful to all the experiences I had as a volunteer. The memory of the gourmet booth's success is what really spurred me on to accept the challenge of taking over a cooking series.

"My schedule is hectic, but I love it. I have never had more energy. It is a good thing, because I need all my waking hours to get everything done. For the first time in years I feel I've got my energies going in the same direction which is far less tiring than being mentally scattered to the four winds. Best of all, earnings are paying for all kinds of marvelous improvements to the house and garden!"

All of us are facing the challenge of finding something to do with our extra years. Many of us are searching out new situations in order to expand our horizons. It is revitalizing to enlarge our capacities to feel, to perceive, to decide, to behave. The hardest choice to put into practice is to go to work. The business world requires more from us than either a volunteer job or an all-consuming interest. We need a new set of credentials to become a professional. We must get ourselves in touch and trained for something which is in demand.

Chapter *V*

"If You Really Want To Do Something, Just Go Ahead and Do It"

A woman's debut as a labor force statistic depends entirely upon the degree to which she has to, wants to, or happens to, become a wage earner. Necessity is a stronger motivation than desire. It is the spur that sends us to an employment agency and makes us dial in answer to a want ad. All considerations of family, schedules, housework, and leisure fade before the task at hand—the need to find a job.

"My last six years have been more like a roller coaster ride than I care to remember. The ups and downs of my life sound like a soap opera. The start of an exciting and glamorous new part-time career was abruptly halted by the emotional and time-consuming wranglings of a divorce. Subsequently I have had to work to support the family, and it is a very different kettle of fish.

"Several years before our marriage went on the rocks I had

found myself with more than enough time on my hands to do what had to be done around the house. Our two older children were in junior high and preferred as little parental attention as possible. The baby was at last in second grade and did not even come home for lunch. I was belligerently saying 'no' to anybody who asked me to do anything. Sometimes I went back to bed in the morning or took a nap. I was more and more tired for no reason. It was obvious I needed to find something to do for my own self-preservation.

"A friend asked me to help out and model some clothes in a fashion show being sponsored by a local woman's club. Since we were all to be inexperienced and untrained, I was not a bit nervous about obliging. Springtime is fashion show time. In the space of a few months I was asked to do two more modeling favors. I was tall, slim, and able to fit most anything. One of the stores whose clothes I had been wearing called to ask if I would come and do a show. I said 'yes,' before the thought of being paid sent a shock wave through my wavering confidence. I was afraid my self-taught poses would be all too obvious by comparison. Luckily, that first show one of the professional models took me aside and gave me a quick fifteen-minute course in how to turn and what to do with my hands and arms.

"In a short time I was as busy as home would allow. I was paid by the show plus an extra fee for fittings. The fringe benefits included clothes and shoes at discount prices and frequent free hair-dos. Since most of the fashion work was done at luncheons, I had my mornings free as well as being home in time for the children. The family's schedule was undisturbed, and I was having a ball! I had drifted into a whole new exciting world. Getting paid was the icing on the cake, which I was able to have and eat as well for awhile.

"There's nothing like a divorce to change your life. The unpleasantries dragged on interminably, and by the time the final papers were drawn my financial circumstances were drastically altered. I came face to face with the realities of having to earn money. My income from modeling was not going to support me and the children. An appointment with an employment agency was inevitable.

"This was an unnerving interview. I managed to turn aside any suggestion of a typing test as if it were unnecessary. My secretarial experience before marriage seemed to satisfy the interviewer. The humiliation of failing a typing test would have destroyed my last shred of confidence. As we discussed the available job possibilities I felt a rising sense of panic. I couldn't bring myself to be trapped into making a fifty-two-week commitment immediately. I knew that I needed a career not just a job, but I also needed time to find what I could do. But I had to have income now. Good fortune and the agency found me a series of temporary jobs.

"It was an ideal way to begin my adjustment to a routine. My typing speed increased a notch with each new job. I found self-discipline I was unaccustomed to practicing. My free time was precious, and I soon realized I could not afford to squander it as I had done in the past. First things were done first and second things probably never. This was a considerable change from the freedom of my modeling days. One insoluable problem was the after-school hours. My youngest could not be left alone, and it was a continuing search for sitters, housekeepers, relatives, long suffering friends, or an older brother or sister to attend. Unhappily there is no child care center within any reasonable distance. I knew that before I could take a full-time job permanently, I would have to find a solution for my own peace of mind, as well as the emotional security of my family.

"I still haven't resolved my problems but in some ways I now feel more confident than I ever did in my life before. I have managed to come through these past difficult years with most of my sanity and good humor intact, which is a major triumph. I know if you want to do anything badly enough you just have to go ahead and do it. My modeling experience was a first hand testament to that. I desperately want to find something to do with my life which is more than just marking time. I need a challenge which can satisfy my ambitions as well as my pocketbook."

The malaise of a woman's middle years has been documented by commentators from Freud to Friedan. Making and remaking beds, and washing and rewashing dishes, stockpiles frustrations to an explosive level. Something's gotta give! Each individual's reaction to this common complaint depends to a great deal on personality. Pent-up emotions have variously been vented in anger, in swallowing pills and alcohol, in overwhelming fatigue and depression, or in compulsive and aggressive behavior. Joining the paid or unpaid occupational world is cheaper than a doctor's couch. Work or something to do is not a panacea to real ills and worries, but being truly busy leaves a good deal less time in which to be upset.

Society agrees that excessive mothering is not the key to producing a generation of well-adjusted children. Even so it is difficult to buck traditions, neighborhood disapproval, and feelings of self-guilt to take on a full working day. "Having to" assuages the guilt and makes allies of both csutom and the community. Recognition of women as a potential untapped resource has directed congressional attention toward federal aid for child day care. The scramblings for after-school supervision are an ever-present burden for those of us who have to work, and a strong deterrent for those who want to.

The distinction between a career and a job lies not in what is being done, but in the amount of commitment with which it is being done. Certainly full-time employment is more of a commitment than part-time, at least in hours worked. However, more important than the number of hours spent at an office is the degree of mental involvement with the task at hand. The choice for a mother who has to work is not easy. She has the option of searching for a career with all the accompanying rewards of expanded responsibilities, higher salary horizons, and increased personal recognition. Or she has the option of finding the job which pays the best money and making the best of it. In either case she has to cope with the limitations imposed by her children's at-home hours and her own individual sense of responsibility to the family schedule.

"Our placid suburban existence complete with one child, stockbroker husband, and busy community-minded wife fell apart overnight. Suddenly, without warning, Charles had a massive heart attack. His first few weeks of recuperation were filled with shock and thinly disguised panic for the future. Finally, the doctor gave him a clean bill of health with virtually no restrictions except for his job. Doctor Holmes quite matter of factly told Charles that commuting was out of the question and that he must find another occupation with less strain. For a brief period we foolishly allowed job problems to eclipse the happy news of regained health.

"We seldom see ourselves in a rut until something happens to jolt us out of it. It is very difficult to consciously go about changing a lifestyle. We had been immersed in our traditional routine, prepared to live pleasantly and uneventfully ever after. Circumstances forced us to spend endless evenings discussing the possibilities of a new career. Once I half seriously suggested that Charlie should become a professional photographer. It was something he did well and had indulged in as a hobby for years. He even built a completely equipped darkroom in the basement. Charlie's eyes lit with the thought, but we quickly dismissed the idea as being too impractical. Financially he needed a job now, and it would take several years to establish himself as a photographer.

"The depth of our rut blinded us to the obvious solution.

It was our thirteen-year-old son who opened our eyes. 'Mother, why don't you work until Dad gets his business going? That would be great, he could come to my afternoon soccer games.' A million reasons immediately came to mind why this idea wouldn't work. It took some soul searching for us to admit to each other that the real obstacle was our own image of respectability. In our world a man goes to business, and a woman stays home. Desperation forced us to consider a different living pattern in spite of our hangups with what people would think or say. We estimated that our savings, together with my salary from a job, could keep us afloat long enough for Charlie to become self-supporting. The first hurdle was cleared, but there were many more to come.

"What could I do after all these years? I had worked before marriage, starting as a secretary and ending up as an office manager for a small company. Unbeknownst to anyone I had been secretly following the newspaper want ads and keeping my ears opened during the last year or so. Many friends were drifting into jobs, and with nobody home all day, I had begun to feel restless pursuing my various odds and ends of activities. However, now that I knew I had to go to work it was an entirely different matter. The pressure to find something returning top dollar was immediate, and I couldn't fuss around with vacation schedules, office surroundings, or prospects for interesting work. I drew up a résumé, such as it was, and marched off to an employment agency.

"It is much easier to find a job when you really need one than when you merely want one. I took the first decent paying position offered, which was an executive secretary in a small architectural firm. Polishing up rusty skills was a breeze compared with adjusting to our new lifestyle. Scheduling dexterity, much patience, and a very large sense of humor on everyone's part were essential. Charlie discovered the mysteries of the washer and dryer between darkroom duties.

Friends eventually stopped teasing him about his gourmet cooking. I learned that being tired is a state of mind, I think. Our small boy found a new friend and a companion in his father."

Society's attitudes toward the role of women have always been more conditional than rational. It is easier to live cross-wise to custom if there is an obvious and pressing reason to do so. Those of us who were married before the 1960's are more likely to observe than experience today's changing values of masculinity and femininity and their role disturbing implications. A new style of living is developing at which most of us can only marvel. However, when circumstances force the issue, "us" have no choice but to hang loose and adjust.

Having to go to work is a must. Wanting to is a maybe. The first step is saying out loud, "I would like to find a job." If no one hears the words it is easy to rationalize not going any further. Once friends and family hear such a thought it is hard to retreat without losing face. It is a hard decision to exchange the executive privileges of motherdom for a boss and a time clock. Working leaves little time for the ladies who lunch or shop or have coffee. It is difficult to abandon the luxury of leisure.

Children and their activities provide a great measure of our own sociability. Often as they grow away from home a disturbing feeling of isolation settles into our lives. To each other we all appear busy and involved with no time to communicate more than superficial thoughts and comments. All of us feel the need for human emotional contact beyond the family. It is a reaffirmation of being someone other than wife and mother. A job offers the opportunity of a shared experience and an antidote for loneliness.

For those of us who have no marketable skill or talent or who no longer cherish the smallest remnant of a dream, finding something to work at is a challenge. The professional world is rightfully leery of a woman who relies on her life experience as adequate job training and who expects to secure a "fulfilling, interesting, challenging job with some responsibility" as a result of bringing up children and chairing a few volunteer committees. It is most difficult for a very competent, highly praised volunteer to find an equivalent paid position. A reputation for "running things" does not necessarily secure an executive job. However, women who have consciously sought proving grounds to develop their abilities through the child raising years will find opportunities available to them. It takes ingenuity, confidence, determination, and family support to find the right one.

"As a volunteer who had taken on more and more commitments, it seemed that I was away from home as much as I was in residence. My latest responsibility had been Coordinator of Education Television Programming on our local station for the Board of Education. My two-year stint had involved gathering props, casting, promotion, advertising, writing scripts, and being general doer of anything. I could feel the letdown coming as my second year drew to a close. My children were all in school and, although it was easy enough to fill my days, I needed something to do which was more challenging. I wanted to see if I could earn money. When I broached the subject to my unsuspecting husband his first comment was 'Whatever for?'

"We went round and round about what I could or would do. Finally he suggested that I investigate the possibilities. At the time I know he felt the whole notion would go away, and I would say 'yes' to some new volunteer project. Even I didn't realize how ready I was to make the break.

"It is very difficult looking for a paying job with nothing but volunteer experience. Many groups will let you hold all kinds of responsible positions gratis but balk at paying a 'volunteer.' I soon discovered that exciting part-time jobs aren't lying around waiting for eager applicants. The best offer I turned up was a low-paying sales job at a nearby shopping mall on the three days of the week I already had variously committed to bridge, garden club, and tennis. What I was giving up was not worth the exchange. Several months went by, and I kept reading the want ads in the local paper. Instinctively I didn't go to an employment agency, because I didn't want to hear the truth, that I wanted to have my cake and eat it too. One day I spotted an ad which read 'Mature woman over 35. Must like people and drive own car.' On a lark I left my youngest with a friend, not telling her where I was going, and went off to answer the ad. I was disappointed to find that it was for a cosmetic firm. I said I wasn't interested. I didn't wear makeup, and, as a matter of fact, I didn't even like it. In spite of my comment I was persuaded to take a few minutes and be made up. Fantastic! I loved the way it felt, and I was amazed by the way I looked. When I went back to pick up my child I was greeted by my friend, 'What in heavens have you done with yourself. You look terrific!' Privately I thought I'd looked pretty good when I left. My reply surprised my own ears more than hers, 'This is a new cosmetic I am thinking about selling. Let me do your face.' I rushed to the car for the samples, and in spite of my inexperience with brushes and creams I produced astonishing results. I had my first customer.

"Before the day was over I had run into several friends around town, all of whom told me how great I looked and wanted to know where they could get some. I know George thought I had flipped when I reported my day's activities including the client waiting list. He was amazed at my eagerness to sell something I had never used nor liked.

"The honest truth was I didn't know the first thing about makeup and at my age felt foolish asking. It was easier to dismiss the whole scene and just use lipstick. It was a revelation to look in the mirror and realize what I had been missing. I was dying to spread the word to my anti-cosmetic friends. The challenge of becoming a professional evangelist was too much to resist. My enthusiasm swept George into agreeing that I should give it a whirl.

"I started as a beauty consultant with a sample case as my only investment. I could still have turned back at any time which gave me the sense of security that I needed to start. I had absolutely no intentions of managing anybody but myself, however within a month I had a staff of four friends working for me. Each came with a special personal reason for working. Business was growing like Topsy, and I just couldn't keep all the inventory in my basement. In any case, I don't think the neighbors would have appreciated a cosmetic sales office next door to them. George and I had not yet resolved my working status, but I had been thinking that I needed a tiny office somewhere in town.

"It was a big decision, and I was still in the thinking stage in my own mind when the director of the territory franchise offered me an associate directorship. The figures showed that in my outstanding first four months I would have made $2,000 more in such a management position. George was completely astounded with the financial success of my venture. He became very enthused with its future possibilities. As my weekend tennis mixed doubles partner, he well knew my love of competition. He couldn't help but recognize that I was on top of the world. His blessing and confidence in my abilities gave me courage to take the directorship. Proudly, I secured a bank loan entirely upon past performance and opened an office. Purchasing inventory was the final commitment, and I felt I was in business for real. I had already given up my bridge and other activities, and now reluctantly my tennis game was the last remnant of my former life to go . . . Strangely enough the children said they like it better now that

I work on a regular schedule. They always know where to find me, and they often drop in my office on their way back and forth."

It is difficult to assess the degree of seriousness of our own intentions. Problems of walking the dog, children's dentist appointments, music lessons, and so forth can be insoluble if we allow them. Often the more time we spend discussing and deciding to do something, the less likely it is to be undertaken. The real test is overcoming our first encounters with defeat and frustration. The rudeness of a secretary is enough to make most of us wonder, if only for a moment, why we left the comfort and security of our domestic world.

For those very few of us who held on to our original dreams of being something or someone, there is no question of what to do with an extra twenty years. The problem is to have confidence and dedication to make it happen. If we want something badly enough our subconscious usually has a way of keeping our conscious mind on the path.

"There is a time and place for everything in our lives. I have come to appreciate this simple wisdom. I have always wanted to be a writer. When I was very young I would tell people that I planned to grow up and be a foreign correspondent. I am not sure where I got the notion, but it stayed with me until high school. The idea of travel to exotic places on exciting assignments must have been reflected from the World War II news blazoned across the front pages. I enjoyed writing in school, even the mundane compositions which were assigned. I had an innate compulsion to publish. For me an unforgettable moment was actually getting a story in print in a children's magazine. Its eight hundred words were read and reread until the magazine pages went limp.

"My visions of publication became dimmed during my years as a college English major. For four years deadlines were a terrible cross to bear. Self-discipline never was my strong suit, and extracurricular activities had a large claim on my time. Marriage followed quickly upon graduation which answered the immediate question of what to do. Three children in four years threw me into a tailspin of fatigue. My tired mind was incapable of much lucid thought, and my book reading slipped into magazine scanning, which required less of my attention. The hitherto unfamiliar world of magazine fiction came into focus. It brought back all my buried desires to appear in print. I thought perhaps I could attempt a short story.

"It was not the right moment in my life. Don and I had finally bought a house and were settling down in the community. I joined several organizations, and all too quickly I was swept up into lots of activities. My time and brain were fragmented more than ever, and the comings and goings of my life did not allow me many undisturbed hours for writing. I had several ideas for stories in my head, but I never could seem to get them going on paper.

"Instead, I devoted myself to writing news releases for the PTA, the church, and all too indiscriminately for any other group who asked. Constant practice was developing my writing skills, but constant deadlines were making me a nervous wreck. One issue of our weekly paper coincidentally turned up five of my publicity stories. At this time the president of an organization for whom I had done several years worth of publicity came to me for advice. She was looking for a professional they could hire to write a special brochure, and she wanted to know if I knew of anyone. I was speechless, furious, and resigned in the same moment. I realized then and there that without pay, I was nobody. I needed to find a job!

"One day I was seized with a sudden burst of confidence, and I made an appointment with the editor of the paper. I marched in and sold him on hiring me as a free-lance feature writer. My first story with a byline was a tremendous thrill even though the subject, 'Recycling Bottles in Suburbia,' was a far cry from my foreign correspondent dreams. The pay was miniscule, but I felt I was a professional. My writing habits began to reflect my new attitude. I was able to sit down in a workman-like fashion and type out stories as assigned. After several years I had accumulated a large scrapbook and a very small bank account.

"Inspired by my reportorial success, I decided seriously to try to break into the free-lance article market. I supplied myself with a wide selection of magazines from the newsstands and an expensive copy of the *Writer's Market*. It took just six months to sell my first article. My determination to succeed gave me self-discipline. I had gained self-confidence through my volunteer writing efforts as well as my newspaper work. It was the right time in my life to become a professional writer."

Holding fast to a dream that was conceived before marriage takes a very tight grip. Family living reshapes our personalities. Over the years our lives move in new and unexpected directions. When we are exposed to unanticipated experiences, dreams can fade from lack of substance. Our freedom to come and go, to be and become, is inextricably bound to our family's demands. Dreams can be destroyed by lack of opportunity. Planning and wishing for something in the distant future without having complete control of the present challenges our self-confidence.

Dreams survive because of and in spite of ourselves. Women are going back to school in ever increasing numbers to prepare for new opportunities or to fulfill credits for careers which have been half forgotten or abandoned since college days. It takes a good deal of self-confidence to register for that first class. The idea of having to compete with much younger students after years away from studies is alternately frightening and challenging. Enrolling in a degree program is a major commitment and anticipates a considerable change in lifestyle. Husband and children must be willing to help mother get through. Homefront support in the face of occasional panic is an essential ingredient to her success.

"The most exciting day of my life in recent memory was my first day at law school. It brought back all the dreams I had growing up. I sat through classes in a daze barely thinking of the husband and four children who would be awaiting my return. Where had all those years gone? In the distant past I had been accepted and ready to enter law school when Chris, a most persuasive young man, convinced me to get married instead.

"For the next fourteen years I didn't have time to regret my choice for a moment. Once or twice I made a stab at extricating myself from the house for a brief fling at several temporary jobs. These were self-indulgences to keep my sanity which were always encouraged by Chris. Since he was the person left solely in charge each time I went to the hospital for another arrival, he was unusually sympathetic to my desires for some time off. A complete change of scene, if only for a few hours a week, does wonders for the housebound spirit. As the years passed, I took several courses at the nearby university which kept my brain in harness. Deep down I guess I never quite put aside my dream of becoming a lawyer. When our four children finally reached an all-day-in-school status, I sent for a law school catalogue.

"Without Chris's full-hearted support I never would nor could have considered such an undertaking. We both understood that even though I was in law school the first order of business would be our family. Perhaps because Chris's mother had been a teacher, he understood my feelings of wanting to have a full-time career when the children were gone. I would not be content with anything less. It took the better part of a year to apply for admission, locate transcripts, and decide on a long-term course of study.

"My first semester I signed up for a single class anticipating much more difficulty than I found in adjusting to the academic world. At home there was no need for realigning chores. I was prepared to run faster and juggle more than ever before, and I was happy to do it. The laundry still was done on time, and the dishes never sat in the sink. The children were proud that mother was in school and took fiendish pleasure in watching me slave over an upcoming exam. I had lots of interesting dinner conversaton which the whole family enjoyed. My exposure to a mixed bag of fellow law students was stimulating and certainly dislodged some of my more conservative views.

"Part-time study can be a long haul and at Chris's urging I have gradually added a few courses each semester. My biggest problem is trying to keep my two lives in proportion. There are moments when I have great effort in focusing my undivided attention on a child's long tale or even an incident in Chris's day. From time to time Chris not unkindly reminds me that a 'B' will do just as well as an 'A' and that our bargain is 'family first.' "

Readiness to enter the marketplace is a state of mind, recognized or not. We just "happen to fall into something" only if we are mentally ready to do so. We are susceptible to the ebbs and flows of the family's emotional fortunes. The age of our children is less of a factor in our going to work inside or outside the house than the current state of tempers, schoolwork, and general well-being. Even the smallest venture into the business world brings about some adjustments in schedules and expectations. If mother is going to shift some of her attention to her own interests, everybody else best be on an upbeat.

Recognition in a public showcase intrigues all of us who have a craft or a talent. Praise from family and friends is always appreciated, and probably without it we would not be encouraged to go beyond the initial stages of an interest or hobby. There does come a time, however, when we need a fresh point of view to sustain our enthusiasm. Selling exposes us to a new critical audience.

"Ever since I was old enough to reach the footpedal on a sewing machine, I have made most of my clothes. My mother and my sisters sewed, so I did as a matter of course. I never truly appreciated having the right fit and design at fractional cost until I was a working bride. It was a budgetary shock to have to shop for clothes. I quite naturally slipped into needle-craft when the children were little, and I was at home with idle fingers. Three boys demanded very little of my dress-making talents. My free time was spent in the kitchen learning to cook. This seemed more important to our existence than making my own wardrobe. Over the years I passed in and out of crewel, embroidery, crochet, bargello, and macramé, but I always came back to needlepoint. I recognized soon enough that the real creativity lay in designing the canvases. In college I had taken art courses and dabbled in paints which came in handy as I tried drawing my own canvases. My first attempts were 'interesting,' as my family so kindly put it, but I did get better with practice. I enjoyed the challenge of creating a design and then finishing a picture with its color and stitch selection. For several years I worked happily away at my hobby in a corner of the family room whenever I had a free moment from the boys and volunteer activities to which I habitually over-committed myself.

"My next door neighbor was an enthusiastic fan of my handiwork. She talked me into donating two especially de-signed hunting scenes to a benefit sale. After they were delivered I had misgivings. What if no one bought them? I was thrilled to be told that not only had they both sold but had brought surprisingly high prices. Bill was pleasantly surprised to discover that there really was a market for such things. Quite unconsciously his attitude toward 'that stuff in the corner' changed. He became an interested critical help in deciding color and design. I still wasn't ready to put a port-folio together and march around selling from store to store. But, it was ego building to know somebody wanted my work.

"Not too many months later good friends opened a needle-work store in town. The word went out that they would take original designs on consignment. I decided I would put a few things in the shop to see if they would sell. Soon I was caught up in the challenge of designing for an unseen buying public, and I worked harder and produced a larger selection than I had originally intended. Bill was as excited and as proud as I when all of mine sold quickly. I was asked to design more canvases, and before I realized it I was in business. I had to abandon my 'do-it-when-I-feel-like-it' work habits and set up a routine. I still liked to work in the family room. Two of the children were in school all day and my nursery school friend kept me company with crayons and trucks. At night it was companionable for Bill to be reading nearby, while the boys came in and out of the room giving free advice.

"Apparently my canvases had a particular appeal, because I rapidly developed a number of stock items the shop wanted in continual supply. Although financially rewarding I did not enjoy the repetition. I loved working on special orders. The designs people wanted were wild. One I poured my heart and soul into was a pillow with the inscription 'I Get No Respect.' In addition I made as many new creations for speculation as time and inclination permitted. My very simple accounting ledger began to fill with entries, and my earnings rose out of the pin money category to the point of raising our income tax bracket.

"One day out of the mail appeared a note from an unknown shop in a distant city asking if I could supply it with four dozen of my valentine pillows. The letter also asked whether I had a catalogue sheet listing my designs. Apparently some-one from my town had come in to the shop with a sample of my work. It was a tempting proposition, not only for the money but for the prestige of branching out beyond the local scene. I had an imaginary glimpse of packaging and selling to department stores and gift shops in cities and resorts throughout the country—of hiring people to paint my original designs to keep up with orders. It was a momentary lapse. I recognized the reality of maintaining my soccer, hockey, and baseball players as well as being an unharassed, unfatigued, and available wife and mother. My letter of refusal went off accompanied with the barest twinge of regret.

"I am fortunate to have found something which I love doing and which is successful. My family thinks mother is terrific. The kids bring friends by to show off my 'work.' I can do as much or as little as I want. There is no need to get involved with mailings, overhead, and more complicated bookkeeping. College for the children and an empty house are still many years off. In this particular stage of my life I am still not ready to give up my weekly tennis game."

It is a jolt to drift into a business operation and come face to face with success. The twin spurs of money and recognition are hard to ignore. It is easy to become more and more involved without giving much hardheaded business thought to the future. A commitment to a job which has fixed hours or a college program which has required courses is definable and can be evaluated in advance. A successful enterprise has a way of snowballing beyond a person's wildest dreams. Suddenly there are questions of profit margins, material costs, available markets, bookkeeping, tax, employees, and who is taking care of the house and children?

Choices of expansion or containment are difficult to make. We must recognize what best suits our family's time demands, our own newly awakened compulsion to achieve, and our desire for extra income. What seemed to "drift" us into a business may be more calculated than we realize. Desire to succeed is a strong motivating force. Once set in motion its energy is hard to restrain.

"Handicrafts have been the pastime of my life. When our children were little and I was a permanent live-in babysitter, I always had a worktable piled high with the pieces of my latest craft. Stacks of magazines with 'how to' articles were hidden around the house under beds waiting for a rainy day. Family and friends came to expect some new and original creation to mark every passing holiday. Despite my grumbles it was fun, and I loved learning how to do new things.

"Several years back when I was looking around for something new to try, I discovered candlemaking. My first attempts looked very home-made with bubbles in the wax and an unmistakable lopsided list. It is much harder to turn out perfect candles than might appear. The more I experimented the more I got hooked on different scents, colors, and varieties of molds. At last I got the hang of the temperature oddities and unmolding process, and I began to create my own ideas. That Christmas I got carried away and designed a personalized candle for all my gifts, everything from a two-foot-high Christmas tree candle to a beautiful sculptured wax fruit basket for a centerpiece. I had outdone myself! A friend to whom I gave the fruit basket was thrilled and begged me to make another one for her mother. I was flattered and agreed to do it, charging the price of materials on her insistence. In no time word got out that I would make candles on order. I had no intention of going into business, but once I said 'yes' a few times I found myself receiving regular requests for parties and special gifts. My husband, Tom, who is a scientist and generally oblivious to most things, was amazed that my home-made-on-the-top-of-the-stove candles were in such demand. He has always been goodnatured about the bits of wax occasionally found in the food, and, as long as things were cleaned up by dinner, he was undisturbed by the cottage industry in his kitchen.

"The local Women's Exchange approached me to sell through it, which I agreed to do even though my profit margin would be less. I preferred selling through a shop instead of from my own kitchen counter. It seemed more professional. Just for fun I entered a craft fair being held in a nearby community. All the exhibitors paid a small percentage of sales to the sponsoring organization, so I had nothing to lose. One of the children went along to help, and her glowing report of our booth's popularity as well as the cash profit in hand greatly impressed the family. As a result of the show a nearby gift shop asked if I could fill a sizable order. Without any thought to what I was getting into I said, 'Yes, of course.'

"Up to this time I had been very casual about my part-time pastime. Orders came in fits and starts and other than during the months prior to the Christmas gift season, I had managed to stay involved with all my other activities. Most of my friends had no idea that I put in as much time as I did, nor did they realize how profitable my so called 'hobby' had become. My bookkeeping was fairly accurate but very informally kept on lots of pieces of paper stuck in a three-ring notebook. Just before tax time and my yearly encounter with Tom, I spent hours sorting and shuffling papers to make my accounts presentable and forestall any longer lecture than usual. When I told him about the shop order he was adamant that I should revise my accounting system before I poured another drop of wax.

"Overnight I streamlined the whole operation, production as well as record keeping. As candlemaking became less of a challenge and more of a business, I raised the prices of my candles from 'bargain inexpensive' to 'boutique exclusive.' For the next six years or so I made literally thousands of candles, occasionally paying teenagers to help package. I had become a regular supplier to many gift shops in the area, which was a convenient way to sell but not as profitable as selling direct. I was often frustrated to find the candles poorly displayed. I never could understand why stores would purchase merchandise if they didn't intend to give it proper shelf space.

"I had a tiger by the tail. I was all out of ideas for candles and tired of wax, wax, and more wax. There was a surprising large income generated by candlemaking, and our family had become accustomed to many enjoyable extras. As if by fate the local gift shop went up for sale, and Judy, a longtime good friend, called in great excitement, 'Hey, why don't we buy the shop and open a Craft Center!'

"For the space of a breath I thought about it and answered, 'Sure, why not. I can arrange my own candles at last.'

"It really wasn't as simple as our telephone conversation made it seem. After my initial snap reaction I did talk to Tom at length, and he encouraged us to work out plans for purchasing the store. I have never in my life put in such a hectic few months. Judy and I became a legally registered corporation, leased the shop, and undertook redecorating and stocking our new Craft Center. No matter what obstacles we encountered, our enthusiasm and ignorance carried us through. There is something to be said for being inexperienced but determined. Nothing could stop us.

"At last we officially opened the Center and friends began stopping in to look or buy. In the beginning we both found it awkward asking them for money. As we became more experienced, all customers merged into 'the public.' Although we quickly acquired several part-time employees, we found that one of us was always needed on the premises. Thank goodness there were two of us. Not only was it more fun than working alone, but we could share responsibilities.

"Our first year was financially more successful than we could have imagined. We had planned on running one or two craft courses on the side, but once we saw the demand, we set up an entire series. The fees from these classes helped. Teaching kept us busier than we liked. We hardly saw our friends except in the store, and we gave up absolutely every extra-curricular activity. Frankly, it was hard enough to find time to cope with home and family. Both our households underwent radical changes in routine. We think nobody seemed to mind too much. However, we suspect our husbands became a little tired of hearing nothing but talk of our Craft Center when they were at parties with us.

"Life's turning points are seldom recognizable. The momentous significance of our decision to open the Center was only apparent by hindsight. I had walked into a full-time career which was unanticipated. None of us, husbands included, had suspected its potentially large income source. These profits made it easier to accept family adjustments which resulted from the job. Our new professional career status was officially recognized when our shop was invited to join the town's heretofore all-male Chamber of Commerce."

It is difficult to change a family's living pattern to conform to the demands of a wife's new job, career, or business undertaking. How much we are willing or able to do so determines how much we can hope to achieve. Whether we need to, want to, or happened to go to work, earning community recognition through our own efforts gives us self-respect and esteem which translates into confidence. Committing our energy, interest, and time to enter the mainstream of society challenges us to rediscover the singular pronoun "I."

Chapter VI

Changing Image

*H*ow well remembered from childhood is the adult admonition, "You will understand when you grow up." The implication was that at some exact time in the future we would be all there was to be. It was a reassuring thought to know that all our insecurities and anxieties would be resolved at some mysterious moment. Nothing is further from the truth. Living is a natural flow of continual change. We can choose to float, swim, or tread water in the swift moving current with inevitable results.

A most significant transformation in most of our lives comes with the realization that our children are no longer dependent on either our physical presence or our mental attention. All those years of purposeful domesticity come to an end, and the role of mother fades from existence. We are confronted with a second lifetime, and the question then is what to do with it?

For most of us until that time the predestination of marriage
and family had controlled our lives with customary restrictions
and obligations. The act of choosing to "do something," to
make a commitment, in itself, gives a sense of having a command over life's forces, of electing to swim.

"Doing something" brings changes in our lives and the lives
of all who touch us. The moment we put ourselves on the line
outside our domestic fiefdom we no longer enjoy the protection and security of family loyalty. We expose ourselves to
being measured by our own merit. Our existence is no longer
dependent on a husband's status, children's progress, and
housekeeping excellence. "I" is liberated from being "only a
woman" and begins to become a person.

Joining the outside world is a risk as well as a challenge.
There is no guarantee of success. It is difficult to exchange
a comfortable or at least familiar status quo for the unknown. Anxiety of failure and fear of criticism are two very
real reasons not to venture forth. It is acceptable to say, "My
husband won't let me work," or "I can't because of the children," or "We just got a new puppy." The truth is we would
like to be useful, constructive, and productive persons. If
we can find the confidence to take the first step, most of us
are willing to take the risk.

Confidence is a fleeting thing, and it takes a myriad of experiences to create a profound respect for what "I" can do.
Unexpected encouragement is treasured. "For the last several
years I had been making paper flower creations on a card
table in a corner of my bedroom. They were perfectly beautiful by my own observations. Local gift shops were selling
them quite successfully. In a moment of confidence I decided
the flowers should be displayed in a large department store.
Before I could think about it I was standing in line on my
assigned calling day, next to an elegant-looking French salesman who was discussing in sophisticated accents with other

salesmen his thousand-dollar stationery orders. I felt sick to my stomach, and I consumed packages of lifesavers as I waited. One of the other men accidentally stepped back on my toe, and I immediately began mumbling apologies for being there and started blithering about my homemade flowers. My look of fright must have struck a gallic spark of kindness and the French salesman asked to see my wares. He proceeded to give me a stern lecture, 'These are nice! Let me tell you something. You have as much right to be on this line as anyone else. You march right in there and show your flowers. You are doing your thing. Show it with style.' I rallied to his words, and when my turn came I pulled myself together and convinced the store to take a substantial order. It was a well-learned lesson in self-respect."

The greatest boost to a faltering ego is an accomplishment achieved in full view of the world "out there." The memory of success of any kind in any endeavor is a building block to confidence. Still, financial reward is the ultimate measure of recognition. People who are paid do not take seriously those who are not. Receipt of the first paycheck initiates us into the marketplace. Knowledge that we are worth something beyond family love and affection is the beginning of a changing image. However, getting used to being somebody takes a great deal of practice.

"As co-authors of two garden books, my friend and I were to appear on a network morning television show. Unfortunately, the taping was rescheduled for a school vacation week. There was nothing to do but bring the four children to the studio before continuing on to the circus matinee we'd planned for months. Everyone enjoyed watching mother being made up, the bright lights and cameras, and most of all meeting some of the other celebrity guests. Several hours later, the morning's activities long forgotten, I was standing in the entrance to Madison Square Garden arguing with my eight-

year-old son not to dig for the crackerjack prize until he was
back in the seat. Whereupon he dropped it, and I found myself
crawling about on my knees looking for it. A woman approached us, I thought to offer her assistance in the search.
However, instead she said, 'Didn't I see you on TV this
morning?' Fortunately I didn't answer the first words which
popped into my head, 'Who me?' Scrambling around the
lobby floor did not make me feel like a gardening expert or
TV personality. A smile and a nod was the best I could
manage. Hunched over the carpet in a circus lobby while
poking among the passing feet is a difficult position from
which to assume the air of a successful authoress."

A marriage certificate is proof of marital status, and a child
verifies motherhood. These roles are easy for us to define and
identify, and we can perform them according to tradition and
example without prompting. There is no prepared script for
becoming a person. It is difficult to know how to behave and
what to demand. "A room of one's own" is the substantiation of
personhood. A bridge table in the corner of a family room is
just not the same. Virginia Woolf's description of eighteenth-
century women novelists writing in their families' sitting
rooms, subject to all kinds of casual interruptions, strikes a
responsive chord in our hearts. Every mother knows a necessary discipline is the ability to work in twenty-minute inter-
vals.

A new image of ourselves begins to come into focus when
we move out of the family room and into a separate space
reserved for mother to do her thing. As we develop a new
dimension in our lives, we must recognize that it will cause a
major shift in our attentions, which can be upsetting to the
delicate balance of family harmony. Everyone expects mother
to be always attentive and available. It is an adjustment to
discover that she has another set of demands on her time and
interest.

A bank account of our own earnings is an additional verification that "I" exists. Spending the funds is not as significant as their depositing. Whether or not the money goes for clothes, college educations, groceries, or a treat for the family, having it to draw on without explaining why is a consciousness-raising experience.

There is a foreseeable risk in changing the traditional image of independent male and dependent female. A wife who seeks the change is responsible for understanding her husband's needs and desires. She must honestly recognize her situational limitations and order her priorities accordingly.

"Since the beginning of our marriage John had worked night and day to build a small printing company into a million-dollar business enterprise over which he presided with dictatorial benevolence. I had for years been his perfect business hostess and convention companion. As a diversion after the children were married, I took up watercolor and earnestly attended weekly classes at the Art Center. At first John was delighted to find me busy and happy with my hobby. In the next several years I developed my style and technique more quickly than anyone thought possible. I amazed even myself. I loved my watercolors and contentedly painted during the weekend hours while John was busy on the phone. I was hesitant to show any of my paintings at the Center. I was still getting used to my new image as a painter.

"Friends had been asking to buy some of my things, but I fended them off by explaining I wasn't good enough yet. I didn't need the money, and it was embarrassing. Still I was flattered to receive such approval. Privately, I had begun to realize that my work was moving out of the amateur class. At cocktail parties John was obviously pleased when people complimented him on my watercolor work, but he always referred to my painting as 'those dabblings.'

"An auction of handcrafted items was scheduled at our

church, and I agreed to donate a large watercolor. The painting turned out superbly, and I was secretly excited to have something I had done at last on public view. For two weeks prior to the auction there was a considerable stir over my picture. When the big night arrived I felt like a runner just before the championship race. They saved my painting for last, and when it was held up John seemed to see it for the first time through a stranger's eyes. He was peculiarly silent throughout the bidding. Unbelievably the price went higher and higher, until, without any warning, John raised his hand to make an extraordinary jump bid. The auctioneer knocked it down to him.

"More angry than I had ever been, I turned to ask why he had bought my picture. Astounded at my reaction he explained, 'I didn't think you really wanted to part with the painting. You don't want some stranger to own it, do you? Besides, the purchase price is tax deductible.'

"It sounds overly dramatic to say, but I think at that moment our entire relationship was in jeopardy. I realized with blinding clarity that John wanted me to himself."

When a woman takes up a new interest to the extent that it becomes a publicly recognized talent, her husband risks losing the person he has been used to knowing. A changing image is a threat to those who are not willing or prepared to expand their experiences during a lifetime. Today's society is encouraging women to seek goals of their own, and most of us are taking advantage of such unexpected support. "The family comes first" is a sacred vow to which we pledge ourselves. This usually means that we rearrange everybody's schedule so that we appear not to be doing too much. Unless we have a full-time job or an office to which we report, our children may not recognize that we are working. The moment of truth comes when the school distributes forms to be completed which ask for mother's occupation. "I" finally becomes someone when a small hand quite unconsciously fills in "writer."

Most of us do not see ourselves as our friends see us, which is probably just as well. As the years go by we collect sets of friends from different activities. Common interests are what bring most of us together. We all see and talk to many people but seldom come to know the whole person. A friend's changing image can threaten or challenge an unchanging status. First impressions are lasting and familiar. It takes time and effort to adjust a friendship in the face of a new image.

"Three years ago I took a part-time job in the public relations department of a museum. Before marriage I had worked there as an assistant to the assistant curator for Oriental Art. Over the years I have kept up my interest and knowledge by taking courses at a nearby college. Quite a while back I started working as a museum volunteer at the reception desk, and through a series of happenings ended up being offered my present spot.

"Aware of my specialty other staff members frequently asked me to take on some of the lecturing chores requested by community clubs and groups, all of whose interests seemed to have turned to the Far East. My working schedule allowed me to continue most of my volunteer activities as well. My friends all vaguely knew that I had taken courses over the years, but since I was still available for lunch and bridge, most people did not understand how involved I was.

"The A.A.U.W. branch to which I belong wrote asking for a speaker from the museum, and I was given the assignment. I must say I was nervous appearing before an audience of friends. From chance conversation I realized that most of them did not fully comprehend my credentials, and, when the president of the club gave me a lengthy introduction, I saw looks of surprise on many familiar faces. With the help of slides I capsulized the history of Chinese art into an hour and ten minutes. At the end of the presentation several friends came over and lavishly praised my lecture. They were all amazed at what I was doing and had done. It really had been no secret, but we were so busy with our own lives that there never seemed to have been time to discuss anything more with them than schools, children, and who is driving where. A few friends were outspoken in their envy of how lucky I was to find such a perfect job. There was no way I could explain to them the hours I had spent studying, when, indeed, I had often wished I could have gone with them on their jaunts. The many, frantic moments I suffered at home trying to prepare for a lecture while simultaneously paying attention to my children, husband, and dinner were never evident from the podium."

Gradual disengagement from complete devotion to homemaking is inevitable as our children grow older and finally leave home. We then face the choice of marking time until retirement or rejuvenating our lives by taking new directions. Individually women are wrestling with the questions "Who am I?" and "Where am I going?" Family and friends are unwitting participants in the struggle through their reactions and their attitudes. What people think of what we do is more of a directing force in our lives than we would like to suppose.

Collectively women of the 1970's are reaching out in all directions to enter the mainstream. Society is being forced to recognize a new image for women. We wish to have control over our own lives after our roles of wife and mother are fulfilled. We seek the influence and authority which our capabilities permit. We want to become people in our own right.

Chapter *VII*

~~~~~~~~~~

"Hello, This Is a Confidence Call..."

A year has come full circle since that day Ann and Marilyn, two cookbook authors–housewives, marched off to the library to learn about women from "then to N.O.W.," and believe us there was a great deal to learn! We have spent those months reading the current literature, and talking to women who are coming to grips with society's changing image of their role and trying to reconcile it with their own needs and desires. It has been an extraordinary experience for us to be allowed to share this mental and emotional process. Along the way we have found new insights into our own lives.

The task of putting ourselves, that is women, into a proper historical perspective was a challenge. Neither one of us had done any research or even serious reading since college days. We spent the better part of three months in the library going through books, periodicals, and bibliographies on the subject of women. Because we live in suburbia, we had difficulty tracing down many of the current materials. So one day we stopped by a paperback store in New York City and bought a large shopping bag full of titles for which we had been searching. We were en route home in a commuter train crowded with tired businessmen, when the weight of the books broke the bag and they tumbled to the floor, titles upwards. Strewn amongst the feet of the astounded men were such headings as *Sexual Politics, A Sexist Society, Supergirls, Sisterhood Is Powerful,* and *A Natural Superiority Of Women.* For a few brief seconds there was a stunned silence as eyes scanned the reading matter on the floor. Then one gentleman began to laugh. We were absolutely mortified, and we both blushed crimson. We tried to retrieve our books, ignoring witty and clever remarks now flying around our ears. Finally, one gentlemen brought down the house with his ringing question, "What are you doing, ladies? Making a revolution?"

Needless to say reading current "Women's Lib" literature did expose us to new and radical points of view. We read psychologists' arguments concerning women's supposed biological destiny and its cultural implications. The history of women's civil and social rights was an intriguing commentary on society through the ages. We plowed through statistical papers describing every detail of women's working and non-working habits. We became conversant with the effect of legislation and laws on women's condition. We discovered the liberation literature and were exposed to sexist philosophy. It was a mind-blowing educational experience!

We were amazed that so much had been written on the subject of women and that we had been completely ignorant of most of the material. It was a rewarding exercise for us to pursue a subject in depth. Before long we experienced the indescribable satisfaction of reading a book and understanding all its author's references. Knowing our brains still functioned gave our confidence a boost. We recognized that most current writers on women were writing from successful professional or academic positions. We realized there is a communication gap between such vantage points and our more ordinary existences. We thought that perhaps we might bridge that gap.

We decided to stop reading and start interviewing other women who we thought may have shared the same experiences as had originally prompted us to write a cookbook. In preparation for this next stage we conducted a series of encounter sessions with ourselves. Many of those were spent laughing at our publishing adventures all over again. Even so, after several days we had pages of notes on the various mental stages we had gone through ever since that dreary day in February when we half seriously considered writing a cookbook.

Introspection is a practice most of us avoid. The apparent inevitability of our lives discourages asking questions which seem to have obvious answers. However, the more we talked with each other and examined our experiences, the more we became convinced that a woman really can prepare a lifeplan which includes marriage, family, and something more. The key is to start the inner thought processes long before it seems necessary or attractive to find something to do in life other than family management. ". . . who am I after all?" is a disturbing question which challenges us to take control of our lives.

We equipped ourselves with a tape recorder, and with a list of provocative questions went in search of subjects to interview. We had decided not to make a big pronouncement about writing a book for fear of sounding too pretentious. Instead, we invented a story about writing a magazine article, which seemed a plausible reason for our new behavior. We soon found that interviewing has more to it than just asking questions. When we played back the tape of our first few trys, all we could hear was the two of us monopolizing a conversation with longwinded questions and explanations. The poor interviewee had considerable difficulty getting her words in edgewise. Before we proceeded further, we made a quick study of selected radio talk shows and learned some valuable tips. We now took time to define our interview objectives and developed a carefully thought out list of questions which we could casually interject into conversation. Most important, we stopped talking and began listening.

We spoke with women of all ages and in all stages of doing their thing. As any soap fan knows, listening to someone talk about her life for an hour is an addicting experience, for her as well as us. Often it was difficult for us to tear ourselves away. As the months passed, our collection of tapes grew, and our book began to take shape. The same sentence fragments continually reoccurred in interviews. It was like a needle stuck in a record groove. "Confidence is a fleeting thing . . . nobody listens . . . I don't ever get tired any more . . . it's a challenge . . . I wish I could do something. . . ."

We had coped with the capriciousness of our own confidence long enough to be sympathetic with anyone else's struggle. It is very difficult for a woman, unaccustomed to projecting herself publicly, to act pleasantly aggressive when really she feels fiercely timid. As we talked with women who were trying their wings, we were always sincerely encouraging. We hoped that we were able to convey our conviction, "If we can, you can." One day we even received a half serious, half joking telephone call from someone we had recently interviewed, and who was about to accept a job, "Hello, this is a confidence call. . . ."

A sense of isolation, even while among friends, is a disquieting phenomenon of the restless world in which we live. Few people listen to the answers to their own questions. Attention spans are short, and everyone is too busy running. Perhaps this explains why so many women welcomed our visits with tape recorder in hand as a rare exception to the superficiality of most conversations. Our obviously sincere interest was so appreciated that several even suggested, "Drop the book idea and become home visitors. We all need someone to talk to."

We knew from our own experiences in trying to maintain a cookbook lecture schedule while putting together a new book that just plain physical energy is an absolute necessity. Stamina is essential for those like ourselves who accept the double responsibility of working and still maintaining a house and home, without rocking either boat. "The faster I run doing something I like, the less tired I am doing those things I must. Scrubbing floors is a breeze when I have interesting thoughts." This sentiment was echoed and re-echoed in our interviews with women who had found their niches in or out of the marketplace.

"If you really want to do something badly enough, just go ahead and do it." These words were repeated to us time and again. Everyone who expressed them understood that behind this simple philosophy lay hours and hours of damn hard work and many disappointments. "Life just seems to be a series of fortunate things falling into place," was a typical understated comment from women who had succeeded. Sheer determination and self-made luck was a common denominator in every case. Good fortune was great but undependable. A source of neverending amazement was the variety of business ventures with which women were involved. "It was a challenge," seems to be reason enough to tackle anything. The message we were receiving loud and clear from everyone interviewed was "Stop the world, we want to get on."

Ever since we stepped on our merry-go-round with the publication of our first cookbook in 1970, we have watched with fascination our public and private metamorphoses. It is difficult to remember who we are to whom, and how to act accordingly. We fade in and out of being somebody or nobody special. A good friend confided to us, "You know, you two aren't any better cooks than the rest of us. You just went ahead and wrote a cookbook."

A most unforgettable and amusing incident explaining our changing image occurred during a lecture tour for our second cookbook, *Ladies Who Lunch*. We were appearing for the third time at a special events program at a large department store. There was a full house with standing room only, and the audience was delighted with our cooking demonstration. Afterward, as we were packing up, one of the publicity assistants said, "You girls are terrific. You and Julia Child draw the biggest crowds, but I think the women enjoy you two best. They can identify with you. After all you aren't really anybody."

The minute the words were spoken, she was undone by what she had said and apologized profusely. We hastened to reassure her that we were not offended. It was in fact a great compliment, because that was exactly the impression we had been working to maintain.

As bright and clever as we had begun to believe we were, there was nothing like an accounting course to knock us down to size. Our yearly hassle at income tax time with both husbands over our inadequate (by their view) bookkeeping procedures finally prompted us to seek out some accounting know-how so that we could take care of these things ourselves. After ten sessions of Bookkeeping for Beginners, we needed a "confidence call."

In the course of our research we attended an all-day N.O.W. convocation which for us was like Alice stepping behind the looking glass. The program was billed to include several prominent names in the women's movement and we were very anxious to hear them in person. Our main concern was not to be spotted as two misplaced suburban housewives.

We spent so much time discussing how we would mingle that we never took time to discuss how we would describe ourselves if asked. We arrived early to reconnoiter. The foyer of the lecture hall was already filled with milling people, all of whom seemed to know each other. Basically we stuck out like sore thumbs. Thankfully no one paid attention to us, and we assembled in the auditorium to hear the introductory speakers.

As we sat listening to the people we had been reading for the past year, their thoughts from the written page took on an emotional life which up to this moment had escaped us. Our publishing and lecturing experiences have been removed from the feminist's arena. Our original challenge was to write a cookbook which was done from the shelter of our kitchens. Storming the barricades of the publishing world took perseverence and ingenuity. In this struggle our protagonist was the front desk secretary. Speaking to suburban women's groups about cooking did not expose us to the harsh realities of male/female competition in business and the professions. We were extremely innocent in the ways of the working world. The inequalities and inequities which women suffer in the marketplace had seemed unfair when we read about such practices, but when we heard about them, the unfairness seemed unconscionable. By the time we were directed to break up into previously selected group discussion, our sensitivity to society's place for women had magnified one hundred fold. We decided to go our separate ways in the morning and meet together for our sandwich lunch to compare notes. Our group experience was self-revealing for us both. When we met for lunch we eagerly exchanged anecdotes.

It seems that in each group the participants were asked to introduce themselves in turn and explain what they did and why they were there. It is very disconcerting to venture into unfamiliar territory, particularly when trying not to be recognized as a fish out of water. We both faced the same horrifying moment when we each had to decide what to say to our particular group when our turns came. In the midst of practicing psychologists, N.O.W. organizers, teachers, writers, and magazine editors, how could we admit that we wrote cookbooks! Unplanned and uncorroborated, we each separately invented a new field of interest for the books we have co-authored. One of us chose Organic Foods and the other Ecology. We had a good laugh at the expense of what we thought had been our raised consciousness. Hopefully no one would confront us with our mismatching co-authorship before the day was through. As emerged as we might appear to our friends in suburbia we both realized from this experience that, as liberated women, we had barely cut the cord.

In spite of a whole year of studying and writing about women's roles, we recognize that our self-image is still a conditioned reflex. One of us had an experience which dramatically illustrates this automatic response.

"I had an appointment with an opthalmologist for a scheduled eye checkup. When I arrived at the office a nurse began taking down the necessary information for the office records. 'Occupation?' she asked. 'Housewife,' I answered without a second's thought or hesitation. Immediately I was appalled to hear what I had said and I motioned to catch her attention. The nurse looked up from her form, puzzled by my agitation. I wanted to protest, 'No! No! Cross that out. I'm really an author.' I realized that my explanation would sound ridiculous. There really was nothing to do but go on to the next question."

As we approached writing this last chapter, the question of an appropriate ending began to plague our thoughts. We had not planned to preach any specific course of action for others to follow. We only intended to provide a confidence boost for those confronting the possibilities of "doing something with their extra twenty years." We wanted to share our exhilaration in becoming more than somebody's wife or so and so's mother, of rediscovering the singular pronoun "I." Our adventures and experiences in venturing beyond the security of a woman's place into the mystique of a man's world have been frustrating, exciting, exhausting, challenging, and hilarious. It has never been dull! We are proof positive of the re-echoing refrain "if you really want to do something badly enough, just go ahead and do it."

For lack of a better solution we finally agreed that inspiration would strike us. In the past this has been our most successful method of coping with writing problems. Admittedly expecting a bolt from the blue to guide our hands and thoughts is hard on the nerves when a publisher's deadline is drawing near. In this case the bolt came from Bamberger's Department Store in New Jersey. The public relations department offered us a job!

Bamberger's offer was not as much of a surprise to us as it was to our family and friends. Over the previous year we had been two of the regular lecturers in a storewide cooking series which the store had staged. In passing, we had become acquainted with the publicity staff. Once we half jokingly said, "If you ever need anybody, just call us." In fact we had several times semi-seriously talked together about taking on a publicity job, someday in the far distant future. We had enjoyed our promotional activities with our cookbooks and had learned a great deal from firsthand experience. Someday it would be fun to try and put into practice the considerable number of notions we had collected during these years.

When a member of Bamberger's public relations department called us for a meeting with the staff, we knew immediately what was in the wind. We arrived nervously at the appointed hour. It was indeed exactly as we feared and hoped, we weren't sure which anxiety was uppermost. We were offered a job.

We left the meeting with conflicting emotions, having explained that we needed a few days to consider the offer. What we really meant was that we needed time to figure out how we could break the news to our respective husbands. We had never mentioned to either one the remotest possibility of taking a job. Also, we both had children who came home for lunch. We had three cats, two dogs, and a mouse between us to be looked after during the day. We both played in a competitive tennis and paddle tennis league. We still had cookbook lectures scheduled. And, the last chapter of our new book was still being written. We were totally unprepared to take on such a commitment.

As it turned out, both husbands were enthused at the opportunity for us to experience much of what we had been writing about. Suddenly, it was we who were beset by misgivings. It was one thing to write about a woman's choices but it certainly was another thing to have to make one. We had been accustomed to a great deal of freedom to come and go even with our lecturing. We had second thoughts about tying ourselves down. Someone once said to us, "My tennis game was the last thing to go," and now we understood exactly what she meant.

Of course we took the job. It would have been out of character to pass up the challenge. However, fulltime employment was impossible considering our family responsibilities and our upcoming book publication. We explained that we could share the job. We would receive one salary, but two of us would be responsible for the demands of the single job. One of us would always be able to cover for family vacations, unexpected children's illnesses, an occasional tennis match, and other such emergencies. This was not our original idea.

Women are just now beginning to come of age in the job market. Traditional work patterns are starting to change. For more than a dozen years, Catalyst, a national organization headquartered in New York City, and devoted to expanding career opportunities for women, has been promoting innovative work patterns. Major companies who want and need the job potential of returning women workers have begun to rethink their traditional employment rules. However, "job sharing" is not an everyday accepted concept. Thanks to a persistent and innovative Bamberger executive we were hired as much as a personnel experiment as needed staff to fulfill a job. For us Bamberger's offered a unique opportunity to pioneer a new hiring policy and prove to ourselves, our employer, and interested bystanders that "job sharing" is a workable and desirable arrangement.

We are thrilled! We have been at work two months and it seems like two days. The biggest hurdle we've found in our new career is trying to explain the idea of "job sharing." We take a certain amount of good-natured kidding from fellow associates about being a vaudeville team and receive tongue-in-cheek inquiries into the state of our soft-shoe routine. Our department head unnecessarily worries whether we can really keep each other informed of what transpires in the other's absence. He should only guess at the number of hours we have spent communicating since our partnership began that rainy day in February.

Ever since that day the tempo of our lives has been double-time. It is impossible to guess what tomorrow will bring, but whatever it is—we're always ready for a new challenge.